794.1   90,794
Pandolfini, Bruce
The winning way: the how, what, and
  why of opening stratagems

DATE DUE
                                12.00

The WINNING WAY

THE HOW, WHAT, AND WHY OF OPENING STRATAGEMS

Bruce Pandolfini

A FIRESIDE BOOK
Published by Simon & Schuster

FIRESIDE
Rockefeller Center
1230 Avenue of the Americas
New York, NY 10020

FIRESIDE and colophon are registered trademarks
of Simon & Schuster Inc.

Designed by Irving Perkins Associates

Manufactured in the United States of America

2   4   6   8   10   9   7   5   3   1

Library of Congress Cataloging-in-Publication Data

Pandolfini, Bruce.
The winning way : the how, what, and why of opening stratagems /
Bruce Pandolfini.
p.   cm.
"A Fireside book."
Includes indexes.
1. Chess—Openings.   I. Title.
GV1450.P298   1998   98-12164
794.1′22—dc21   CIP

ISBN 0-684-83949-0

ACKNOWLEDGMENTS

I would like to thank chess master Bruce Alberston for his helpful analysis of all the examples, and my editor, Diana Newman, for her expertise, care, and energy in overseeing the entire project.

For my favorite student

CONTENTS

♚

INTRODUCTION

♛

The Winning Way is about winning chess games—quickly, in the first ten or twelve moves. In this sense it's an opening book, presenting variations by standard beginning moves. To win quickly, you need to rely on tactical maneuvers—sudden attacks and threats such as forks, pins, and skewers. So *The Winning Way* is also about tactics. I trust you will find it handy to have both an opening book and a tactical book in this compact volume.

There are other books of short games that sort material according to opening, class of tactic, or both. What distinguishes *The Winning Way* from these is its chief method of classification, which is to emphasize the actual winning move rather than the category of that move.

This book does refer to standard categories, such as the names of openings. But since opening lines can diverge enormously within the first few moves, the same names can indicate totally unrelated variations. These terms (Queen's Gambit, English Opening, etc.) therefore reduce to mere words, providing no special aid to students who are trying to assimilate winning techniques into their own play. For this reason, because they lack specificity, the names of openings have not been made integral to *The Winning Way's* organization.

Nor does this book place great emphasis on the class of tactic used, such as forks or pins. Just as the names of openings have dubious educational value, it's questionable how truly helpful it is to clump stratagems into tactical groups. There are many different types of forks, and their relation may be tangential at best. No, for students who really wish to put into practice what they read—most of us only have so much time—it makes little sense to pore over amorphous, shapeshifting generalities that can't be applied in practice. (Try it. See how far you get.)

This is where *The Winning Way* comes in. Rather than underscoring unrelated moves whose only connection is that they fall into the same overall class, it groups tactical ideas by the same specific winning move. Thus, by learning a particular move, the reader also develops familiarity with all the connective routes and target squares, all the ploys and ruses, that lead up to it. Most chess instructors know that concrete moves, shown over and over, can be memorized for actual use, whereas generalities and platitudes don't make the same impression. General ideas can be remembered, but they don't usually help when you're trying to find your next move.

To this end, *The Winning Way* delivers about twenty of these strong, particular moves. They form the bedrock of the book, and the book's message is clear: Learn these moves and you will be armed to the teeth in your own personal battles for chess supremacy.

These winning moves are listed in ten chapters. Some chapters focus on a single move, others on several, and each chapter contains eight or more examples. There are 150 examples in all, presented one per page, with each introduced by a descriptive phrase that encapsulates the winning method.

These descriptive phrases are cardinal to the instruction. In uncomplicated, sometimes colorful, language, they emphasize just the necessary information in a manner that's easy to recall. In fact, as a handy review, I recommend turning from caption to caption, trying to quickly remember what each phrase signifies. By repeated study, these captions can become convenient reminders, alerting students to winning moves and methods in their own games. For instance, consider example number two, whose phrase is **"Qh5+ forces the king to move."** This suggests that if you want to force the enemy king to move in your own games, so that your opponent thereby loses the right to castle, you should be on the lookout for opportunities to give a queen check on h5 (or h4 for Black), when the queen is safe and the check can't be blocked.

Just below the caption, on the left, comes the name of the opening (see, you get this anyway). To the right of the opening name is a set of moves in algebraic notation to introduce the opening variation. Play these moves out and you will arrive at the position in the diagram that appears underneath the opening moves.

The diagram illustrates a situation just prior to a strong move. You should try to visualize this move being played on the board, then turn to the next section down the page, titled "Winning way." Herein lies the answer to the problem, including the key move and a light analysis. In most instances, the move to be used is implied by the caption at the top, as well as by the chapter itself. For example, the second chapter revolves around the move Qa4 (Qa5 for Black), so there's a good chance that this move is paramount to the diagram. (One proviso: Some chapters offer several related moves, so the answer is not always automatic.) Finally, the last section on the page, "How, what, and why," explains what happened and what to look for in your own play.

In addition to the ten chapters of related winning moves, you will find several appendices at the back of the book that classify the material by openings and general tactics. These will be helpful if you also want to follow a more traditional approach to your studies. And don't overlook the final appendix, covering lines of attack. It offers a means to study stratagems that capitalize on the same key ranks, files, and diagonals—to my knowledge, a methodology of classification tendered in no other chess book.

That's it—not hard to understand, and really easy to exploit for your own use. How should you proceed? Just get to it. Start with section one, example one, and begin working your way through. And when you get back to your own play, see if at least some of these winning moves don't pop up. There's nothing like taking new ideas and making something of them, especially those that help you win real chess games.

HOW TO READ CHESS MOVES
IN ALGEBRAIC NOTATION

♛

To understand algebraic notation you must view the chessboard as an eight-by-eight grid. Every square on the grid has its own name, based on the intersecting file and rank.

Files, the rows of squares going up and down, are lettered **a** through **h**. Ranks, the rows of squares going across, are numbered **1** through **8**.

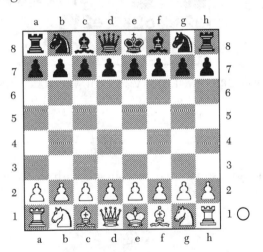

THE STARTING POSITION

Squares are designated by combining those letters and numbers. For each name, the letter is lowercase and appears first, before the number. Thus, in the diagram of the starting position, White's queen occupies **d1** and Black's **d8**.

There is only one perspective in the algebraic system: White's.

All squares are named from White's side of the board. For example, the a-file is always on White's left and Black's right. The first rank is always the one closest to White and farthest from Black.

The algebraic grid below gives the names and positions of all the squares. You might find it helpful to photocopy it and use it as a bookmark so it's always there as a reminder.

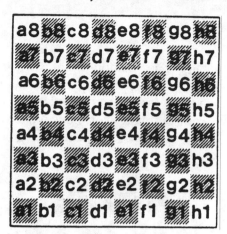

THE ALGEBRAIC GRID. EVERY SQUARE HAS A UNIQUE NAME.

Other Symbols

You should also familiarize yourself with the following symbols:

Symbol	Meaning
K	king
Q	queen
R	rook
B	bishop
N	knight
P	pawn (not used in algebraic notation)
-	moves to

Symbol	Meaning
x	captures
+	check
#	checkmate
0-0	castles kingside
0-0-0	castles queenside
!	good move
?	bad move
!!	brilliant move
??	blunder
!?	probably a good move
?!	probably a bad move
e.p.	en passant
1-0	White wins
0-1	Black wins

Note that though **P** stands for pawn, it is not used in algebraic notation (though it is used in descriptive notation, which is not necessary for this book). If no indication of the moving unit is given in algebraic notation, the move is a pawn move.

BEFORE YOU START

♛

Bear in mind that, under comparable conditions, what succeeds for White also works for Black. Thus if a tactic hinges on White playing the queen to d4, a similar tactic for Black would require playing the queen to d5. (Just remember that in algebraic notation Black's pieces start on the higher numbers. White's begin on the 1st and 2nd ranks, Black's on the 7th and 8th.) While we have provided a fair number of stratagems for White and Black, each example actually applies to both colors. So if a winning shot is given from the Black perspective, remember that in your own games you may find the opportunity to play an analogous tactic for White.

♔

CHAPTER ONE

Qh5/Qh4

Our first section contains eighteen examples based on winning by moving the queen to king-rook-five. In algebraic notation, that's Qh5 (queen to h5) for White and Qh4 (queen to h4) for Black. From this square (h5 for White, h4 for Black) the queen is in line to diagonally attack (along the e8-h5 diagonal for White or the e1-h4 diagonal for Black) the uncastled enemy king on its original square. If the opponent has castled kingside, the queen can fuel a deadly kingside attack. So positioned, the queen also assails points across the fifth rank (the fourth for Black) and along the conjoining h-file. Most of the situations lead to checkmate or the issuing of a winning double attack by hitting the king and other opposing units along the connective routes.

BISHOP'S OPENING   **1.** e4   e5   **2.** Bc4   Be7

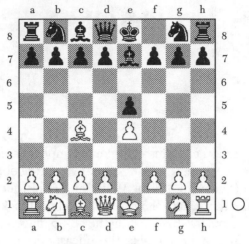

WHITE TO MOVE

Winning way: The queen sortie **3. Qh5!** gives a double attack, to f7 and e5. Black will have to stop the mate, say by moving the pawn to g6, and White then takes the e-pawn for free.

How, what, and why: Black's second move is a mistake. In playing the bishop to e7, the defender is thinking too defensively. Such passive play is uncalled for, and by blocking e7, Black is unable to move his queen to that square in order to guard f7. The backbreaker is White's aggressive bishop at c4, poised to combine with the queen to usurp f7.

2   Qh5+ forces the king to move

CENTER GAME   **1.** e4   e5   **2.** d4   f6   **3.** dxe5   fxe5

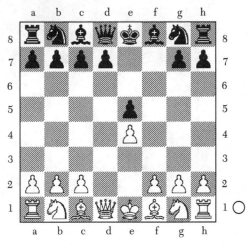

WHITE TO MOVE

Winning way: White scores with **4. Qh5+.** Black must move the king to e7, for blocking with the g-pawn loses the rook at h8 to White's follow-up queen check at e5. So White gains the king-pawn with check, and Black is in big trouble.

How, what, and why: Black neglects development, opting to defend the menaced e-pawn the worst way, with the f-pawn. This exposes the e8-h5 diagonal. But White needs a second target (the other is the king), so he exchanges in the center to fix the weakness at e5. This is essential, for if the e-pawn is not capturable for free, White's queen check at h5 is not a true fork and fails to win anything. In fact, it would only waste time, for Black could block the check with g7-g6, forcing the queen to withdraw without any gain. Thus, if White checks at h5 on the second move instead of the third, he winds up throwing away the initiative.

3   Qh4+ wins the cornered rook at h1

KING'S GAMBIT DECLINED   **1.** e4   e5   **2.** f4   Bc5   **3.** fxe5??

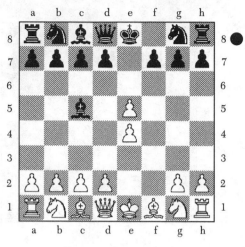

BLACK TO MOVE

Winning way: The finishing move is **3. . . . Qh4+.** If White moves the king to e2, the queen takes on e4 and it's mate. So, in order to avert mate, White must make a huge concession and play 4. g3. This loses the rook at h1 by 4. . . . Qxe4+.

How, what, and why: Black declines the gambit, introducing the king-bishop to c5, so that it cuts across the center, deep into the heart of White's camp. The best third move for White is to develop the king-knight to f3, where it guards the sensitive square h4 and gets off the bishop's line of attack. But taking the king-pawn, 3. fxe5??, loses immediately. It doesn't protect against the queen check at h4 and actually opens up the fourth rank, giving Black's queen a red carpet to the unprotected e4-pawn.

4   Qh5+ forces g6, which can be taken

OWEN'S DEFENSE   **1.** e4 b6 **2.** d4 Bb7 **3.** Bd3 f5
                        4. exf5 Bxg2 **5.** Qh5+ g6 **6.** fxg6 Nf6

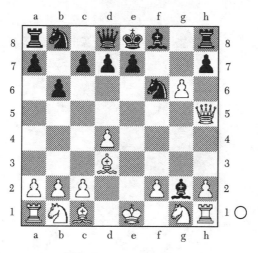

WHITE TO MOVE

Winning way: The terminator is **7. gxh7+!**. Black's knight must take White's queen, and a version of the Fool's Mate (an unblockable check on the e8-h5 diagonal) ensues with the bishop's entry to g6.

How, what, and why: Eyeing White's rook at h1, Black riskily moves the f-pawn, trying to lure the e4-pawn off the b7-g2 diagonal. This exposes Black's king to a queen check at h5, and though the check can be blocked, White's f-pawn is able to capture the g-pawn. At this point, White threatens discovered mate by any movement of the g-pawn. Black attempts to shoo away White's queen, forgetting that once the h-pawn is taken, White doesn't need the queen to mate, for the bishop can fulfill the same function by occupying the wide-open e8-h5 diagonal at g6.

5   Qh5+ forces g6 with Bxg6+ to follow

CARO-KANN DEFENSE   **1.** e4   c6   **2.** d4   d5   **3.** Bd3   Nf6
              4. e5   Nfd7   **5.** e6   fxe6

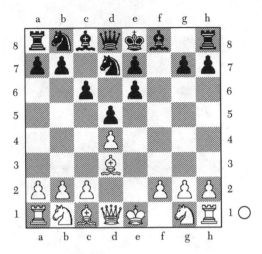

WHITE TO MOVE

Winning way: There's an end in sight via **6. Qh5+.** After the requisite block on g6, White mates in two moves by taking on g6 with either the bishop or queen and then retaking with the remaining piece.

How, what, and why: Black misses an opportunity on the third move. Instead of developing mechanically, he should exchange pawns. After White takes back with the bishop, Black could then develop the king-knight with a gain of time. Invigorated by Black's oversight, White uses the still extant e-pawn to advance on the knight, turning the attack back on the opponent. Black retreats the knight to a stuffy position at d7, leaving the Black king gasping for air. The final failure is taking the e-pawn once it moves to e6. This punctures the e8-h5 diagonal, and White's queen grabs the chance, checking at h5 and hooking up with the bishop at the g6 crossroads.

6 Qh4+ forces g3, and the knight on e4 can take

DORY DEFENSE 1. d4 Nf6 2. c4 e6 3. Nf3 Ne4
4. Nfd2 Bb4 5. a3 Qf6 6. f3 Qh4+
7. g3

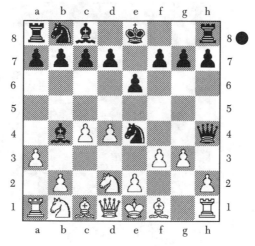

BLACK TO MOVE

Winning way: White loses after **7. . . . Nxg3!.** The intrusive knight menaces the rook at h1, which is lost anyhow, for the h-pawn is pinned by the queen. But to take the knight is suicide, for Black's queen takes back with a Fool's Mate.

How, what, and why: White's withdrawing knight move to d2 is designed to get rid of Black's knight. He should follow with 5. Qc2, but instead pushes the a-pawn, weakening his position and wasting time. White then tries to defend f2 by scaring off the e4-knight with the f-pawn, which bares the e1-h4 diagonal. A queen check follows at h4. White blocks at g3, and Black's knight busts through, taking the g-pawn and accosting the rook. Instead of trying to clear some room for the king, however, White takes the knight and is mated at g3. Note that if the White knight stays at f3, the Black queen moves to f6 and h4 would both flop. The f-file would remain blocked, and h4 would still be guarded.

7   Qh5+ and Nxg6 is repulsed by Qxe4+

DAMIANO'S DEFENSE   **1.** e4 e5 **2.** Nf3 f6
                     3. Nxe5 Qe7 **4.** Qh5+ g6 **5.** Nxg6

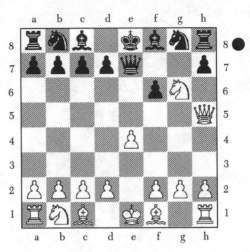

BLACK TO MOVE

Winning way: Black counters with a forking queen check, **5. . . . Qxe4+.** No matter how White gets out of check, Black adds the g6-knight to his trophy case.

How, what, and why: White naturally is encouraged to be aggressive after Black's weak f-pawn move. But the queen check at h5 fails in this case. It looks strong because of the pin on the h-pawn, but White overlooks the ideal defensive position of Black's queen, which can stop the action by capturing on e4 with check. The free move that Black gets forcing White to move out of check, and the forking centralization, turn the once peerless g6-knight into a sitting duck.

6. Qe2 pinning Black's Queen and saving White's Knight
7, no

BRUCE PANDOLFINI

8   Qh5+ and Ng6+ wins the exchange

ALAPIN'S OPENING   **1.** e4   e5   **2.** Ne2   f6   **3.** f4   exf4
4. Nxf4   Bd6   **5.** Qh5+   Kf8

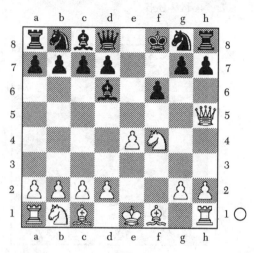

WHITE TO MOVE

Winning way: White garners the exchange (a rook for a minor piece) by **6. Ng6+.** This move forks the king and the confined h8 rook. Black's best response is to chomp the knight, and White's queen takes the rook, a gain of approximately two points.

How, what, and why: Once again, the weakening f-pawn move proves costly. Here it appears that Black can get out of check by moving his king. Otherwise he'd have to block with the g-pawn, which could then be captured by the f4-knight with impunity because of the queen's pin. But even with nothing on g6, White's knight goes there with advantage, for the pin on the h-pawn exists nonetheless. Note that the same knight check succeeds whether Black's king is on e7 or f8.

RUY LOPEZ   **1.** e4   e5   **2.** Nf3   Nc6   **3.** Bb5   a6
             4. Bxc6   dxc6 **5.** 0-0   f6   **6.** d4   exd4
             7. Nxd4   Bc5

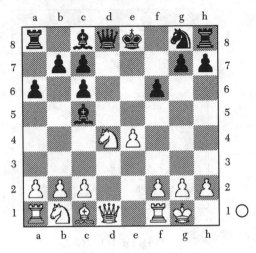

WHITE TO MOVE

Winning way: Black seems to gain time for development by attacking White's d4-knight, but it's White who gains time and more, expropriating the c5-bishop with the fork **8. Qh5+**. Regardless of how Black deals with the check, White eats the bishop without any indigestion.

How, what, and why: This is, a normal line in the Exchange Variation (4. Bxc6) of the Ruy Lopez. Black's f-pawn advance does not lose here. Rather, it's the flub on the seventh move that fails. As a rule, when the fifth rank is clear, be careful about placing the king-bishop on c5 if the f-pawn has moved, especially to f6. A queen check could cost you.

10   Qh5+ and Qxc5 are set up by taking on e4

RUY LOPEZ   **1.** e4   e5   **2.** Nf3   Nc6   **3.** Bb5   Nf6
4. 0-0   Nxe4   **5.** d4   exd4   **6.** Re1   f5
7. Nxd4   Bc5

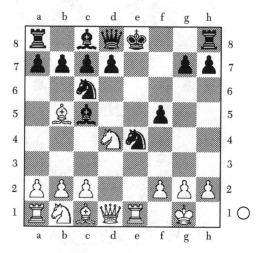

WHITE TO MOVE

Winning way: White breaks through with **8. Rxe4+.** After Black takes back with the f-pawn, cleaning out the fifth rank, White's queen checks at h5 and picks up the bishop on c5 next move. Thus, White barters a rook for two minor pieces.

How, what, and why: To guard the knight on e4, Black advances the f-pawn two squares. This blocks up the fifth rank, so that a queen check at h5 does not attack c5 directly. In some similar cases, the defender can cope with Qh5+ merely by blocking with the g-pawn. So White sacrifices the exchange, realizing that when Black recaptures on e4, he exposes the c5-bishop along the horizontal row. A queen check at h5 is then a fork, and the bishop dies in ignominy.

11   Qh5+ wins on c5 after exchange on e6

MAX LANGE ATTACK   **1.** e4 e5 **2.** Nf3 Nc6 **3.** Bc4 Bc5
4. d4 exd4 **5.** 0-0 Nf6 **6.** e5 d5
7. exf6 dxc4 **8.** Re1+ Be6
9. Ng5 Qxf6

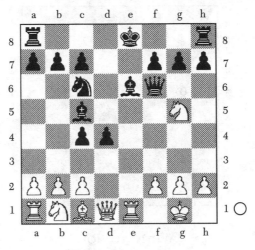

WHITE TO MOVE

Winning way: The blinds are opened by the blunt **10. Nxe6.** If
Black takes back, 10. . . . fxe6, which is the natural retort, attempting to maintain material balance, White checks on h5 with
the queen, adding the c5-bishop to his cache a move later.

How, what, and why: In this wild position, which is an old book
trap, Black gets the pawns and White obtains clear lines for
attack, most notably the open e-file and the queen's unblocked
channel to h5. Still, after the rook checks at e1, the e-file is
stopgapped by the bishop at e6. Moreover, the f-pawn remains
on its original square, f7, keeping the e8-h5 diagonal zippered.
The knight's intrusion to g5, and the follow-up capture on e6,
change all that, and the c5-bishop winds up back in the box.

Qh4+ wins on d4

FRENCH DEFENSE   **1.** e4   e6   **2.** d4   d5   **3.** e5   c5
                 4. c3   Nc6   **5.** f4   f6   **6.** Nf3   fxe5
                 7. fxe5   cxd4   **8.** cxd4   Bb4+
                 9. Bd2   Bxd2+   **10.** Nbxd2

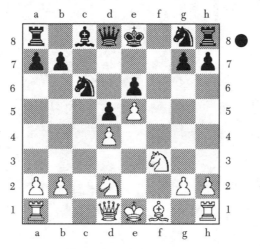

BLACK TO MOVE

Winning way: The d-pawn is pilfered by **10. . . . Nxd4.** White can take the infiltrator with the f3-knight, but a Black queen check at h4 ensues. White ends the check and Black gets the d4-knight with his queen. Black has won a pawn, and the damage is not over.

How, what, and why: The problems set in for White with the unnecessary and quite risky advance of the f-pawn. A wiser policy is the simple development of the king-knight to f3. This secures the center adequately without incurring the integral difficulties that stem from overextensive pawn moves. White's final error is taking back on d2 with the queen-knight instead of with the queen. This recapture looks as if it builds White's game, but actually it obstructs the queen's defense of d4. A simple exchanging combination follows, and the d-pawn vanishes.

QUEEN'S GAMBIT ACCEPTED
1. d4   d5   **2.** c4   dxc4
3. Nf3   Bg4 **4.** Ne5   Be6
5. e4   f6   **6.** Qh5+ g6
7. Nxg6 Bf7

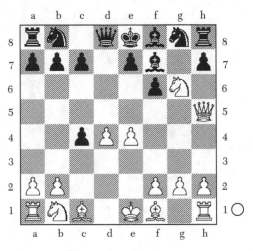

WHITE TO MOVE

Winning way: White's queen extricates itself from the pin by **8. Qb5+.** If Black blocks the check with the c-pawn, the queen takes on b7. However Black responds, White is going to acquire at least the exchange (rook for minor piece) by capturing one of the rooks.

How, what, and why: Whenever the c8-bishop moves early, the b7-pawn is unprotected and therefore vulnerable. A typical way to shoot at it with the Black king still on its original square is to shift the White queen from h5 to b5 with check (the queen also tends to come from e2). Here, this transfer is particularly propitious because it enables the queen to escape the pin with a gain of time, so that Black is unable to take the g6-knight without first replying to the check. In the end, White wins by delivering and maintaining double threats.

Caro-Kann Defense   **1.** e4 c6   **2.** d4 d5
              3. Nc3 dxe4   **4.** Nxe4 Nd7
              5. Ng5 h6   **6.** Ne6 Qa5+
              7. Bd2 Qb6   **8.** Bd3 fxe6

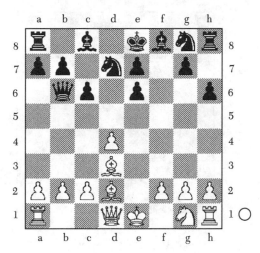

WHITE TO MOVE

Winning way: White wins big with **9. Qh5+.** If Black blocks the check with the g-pawn, White's bishop takes and renews the threat, forcing the king to d8. The king could also move to d8 directly, without first blocking. In either case, White pins and wins the Black queen, placing the dark-square bishop on the protected square a5, guarded by the queen on h5.

How, what, and why: The impetus for White's onslaught is Black's pawn move to h6. This advance attacks the knight, though it weakens g6. White tries to blow away the rest of the e8-h5 diagonal's shelter by a diverting knight sacrifice on e6. Black gains salvaging time by checking on a5 and repositioning the queen to swipe at b2. But Black winds up accepting the proffered e6-knight, and White wins the queen by checking on h5 in order to support a pinning lance on a5.

HUNGARIAN DEFENSE   **1.** e4   e5   **2.** Nf3   Nc6
                  3. Bc4   Be7   **4.** d4   exd4
                  5. c3   Nf6   **6.** e5   Ne4   **7.** Bd5   Ng5

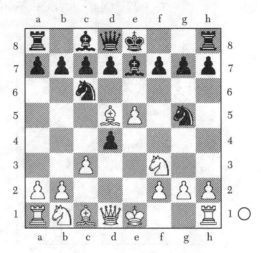

WHITE TO MOVE

Winning way: White augments the score by **8. Nxg5.** After Black takes back with the e7-bishop, White's queen invades on h5, threatening both the bishop at g5 and mate at f7. To thwart the mate threat, Black must forsake the dark-square bishop.

How, what, and why: Black's quiet third move is designed to control g5, especially against the intrusion of a White knight. But in allowing his king-knight to be driven from f6, Black renders h5 quite inviting to the enemy queen. It appears at first that the queen's path to h5 is blocked by the f3-knight, but a simple exchange on g5 unblocks the line and leads to chessic disaster.

16 Qh4+ guards against intrusion on h6

KING'S INDIAN DEFENSE   **1.** d4   Nf6   **2.** c4   g6
3. Nc3   Bg7   **4.** e4   d6
5. f3   0-0   **6.** Be3   e5   **7.** d5   Ne8
8. Qd2   f5   **9.** Bh6

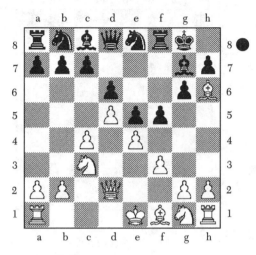

BLACK TO MOVE

Winning way: Black seems to be on the defensive, but not in reality, for **9. . . . Qh4+** turns the point of view. It's a double attack, and after White gets out of check, Black can capture White's bishop on h6 for zilch.

How, what, and why: Here we see typical strategies. White tries to trade off bishops to weaken Black's kingside, and Black aims to attack at the base of White's pawn chain (e4) by the thrust f7-f5. But it's White's king that's exposed along the e1-h4 diagonal, and it's easy to overlook that a queen check at h4 can defend along the h-file, going backward to safeguard h6. Black's invasive queen is omnipresent.

Qe5+ centralizes the attack

RUY LOPEZ   **1.** e4   e5   **2.** Nf3   Nc6   **3.** Bb5   Qf6
4. Nc3   Nd4   **5.** Nxd4   exd4   **6.** Nd5   Qd8
7. Qh5   c6

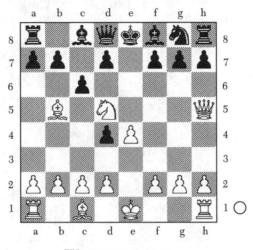

WHITE TO MOVE

Winning way: White's queen dominates from the central over-look with **8. Qe5+.** Black's best retort is to block with the bishop at e7. Even though White's bishop and knight are forked by the pawn on c6, he comes out ahead materially when his queen gobbles the g7-pawn, menacing the h8-rook.

How, what, and why: Sometimes planting the queen on h5 is not done for immediate tactics so much as to exert annoying pressure, including the option of shifting to the center for total dominance. Note that after White's queen checks on e5 in the diagram, Black cannot block on e7 with the g8-knight, for White then checks on c7 with the d5-knight and Black must surrender his queen. Using h5 as a base to transfer to a domineering position is a typical winning motif.

18 Qh5 combines with bishop and knight to win on f7

GIUOCO PIANO **1.** e4 e5 **2.** Nf3 Nc6 **3.** Bc4 Bc5
4. d3 Nge7 **5.** Ng5 0-0 **6.** Qh5 h6
7. Nxf7 Qe8

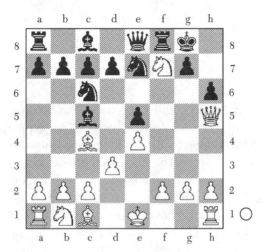

WHITE TO MOVE

Winning way: White mates with **8. Nxh6+**. This gives double check and forces Black to scurry with his king to the h-file. White's knight then jumps back to f7, uncovering check from the queen. The king retreats to g8 and White's queen, protected by the f7-knight, mates on h8.

How, what, and why: Black's troubles set in after the bleak developing move of the king-knight to e7. At e7, instead of the more natural perch, f6, the knight does not protect h7 and h5. This renders h5 accessible to White's queen, which can enter the scene with a double threat to f7 and h7 whenever there's a supporting knight on g5 and bishop on c4. As a rule, prefer placing the knight on f6 to putting it on e7. It's more aggressive and wards off these possibilities.

CHAPTER TWO

Qa4/Qa5

In this second section, the key move also involves the queen, moving it to queen-rook-four, which is Qa4 (queen to a4) for White and Qa5 (queen to a5) for Black. On queen-rook-four, the queen is placed to attack the uncastled enemy king on its original square along the a4-e8 diagonal (or the a5-e1 diagonal for Black), combining this assault with correlating aggression along the fourth rank for White (the fifth rank for Black) and the a-file. Unlike the previous chapter, where many of the onslaughts lead directly to mate, here the chief way to win is through some form of double attack. For instance, a White queen may be able to move to a4, checking the Black king at e8 while also menacing a Black bishop stationed at b4.

19   Qa4+ wins the bishop on b4

QUEEN'S GAMBIT DECLINED   **1.** d4   d5   **2.** c4   e6
                           3. Nc3   Nf6   **4.** Bg5   Bb4
                           5. e3   Nbd7   **6.** Bxf6   Nxf6

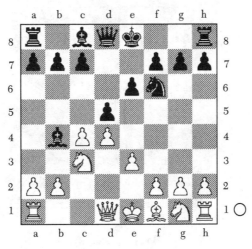

WHITE TO MOVE

Winning way: The gain is immediate and decisive. White forks the opposing king and bishop by **7. Qa4+.** No matter how Black replies, White's queen plucks the hapless bishop.

How, what, and why: Whenever the c-pawn moves early, the queen has access to the queenside along the a4-d1 diagonal (the a5-d8 diagonal for Black). The result is that the queen can often move to a4 with a forking check, swiping at additional points along the fourth rank and the a-file. The villain here is Black's sixth-move take-back on f6, which unnecessarily opens the a4-e8 diagonal. Black should recapture with the queen, not the knight. He could also save the b4-bishop by taking the c3-knight with check before retaking on f6. Either of these work.

Qa4+ wins on b4 or c6

CATALAN OPENING   **1.** d4   d5   **2.** c4   e6   **3.** g3   b6
4. cxd5   exd5   **5.** Nc3   Bb4

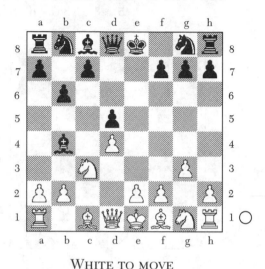

WHITE TO MOVE

Winning way: White wins with **6. Qa4+,** forking the king and b4-bishop. Black can save the bishop by blocking on c6 with the knight, but that merely substitutes the loss of one minor piece for another, as White's queen takes on c6 for free.

How, what, and why: Sometimes the check on a4 can be dealt with by blocking on c6 with a knight, saving the b4-bishop. This counter seldom succeeds, however, if c6 is weakened by b-pawn advance. Black's first mistake is to enfeeble the queenside light squares by pushing b7 to b6, which makes the second error, developing the bishop to b4, a real lemon.

21 Qa4+ forces Nc6, which can be taken

CATALAN OPENING **1.** d4 d5 **2.** Nf3 Nf6 **3.** c4 Bg4
       4. Ne5 Bf5 **5.** g3 h6 **6.** Bg2 e6
       7. 0-0 Qc8 **8.** Nc3 Bb4

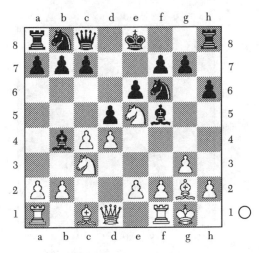

WHITE TO MOVE

Winning way: Black's last move is punished by **9. Qa4+**. If Black blocks with the knight on c6, White's knight takes Black's. And if Black then tries to salvage the hanging bishop by taking on c3, White retreats the c6-knight to e5, unveiling a check from the queen that insures material profit.

How, what, and why: Developing the bishop to b4 is an outright blunder, but Black was already going astray. While Black wastes time guarding b7, White uses the tempo to castle. If White remains uncastled, Black might be able to save the b4-bishop, inserting a capture on c3 with check before recapturing on c6. But alas, White is safely castled when the hit occurs.

22   Qa4+ forces Nc6, which loses to d4-d5

PONZIANI OPENING   **1.** e4   e5   **2.** c3   Bc5   **3.** Nf3   d6
4. d4   exd4   **5.** cxd4   Bb4+
6. Nc3   Nf6   **7.** Qa4+   Nc6

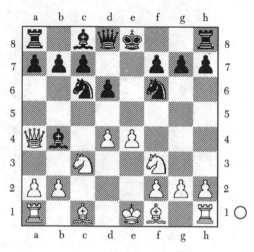

WHITE TO MOVE

Winning way: White cashes in on the pin with **8. d5.** Black can save the b4-bishop by taking on c3 with check. But after White takes back, Black cannot break the pin on the c6-knight in time to come to its rescue. The d5-pawn gets it.

How, what, and why: Black is actually able to uphold the b4-bishop, but at a cost: He must submit to a pin on the c6-knight. While White cannot capture the knight at once, the pin along the a4-e8 diagonal incapacitates it. White's d-pawn advances and reduces it to Silly Putty. What was Black's losing bungle? Omitting to exchange bishop for knight on move six.

SICILIAN DEFENSE   **1.** e4   c5   **2.** d4   cxd4   **3.** Nf3   e5
             4. Nxe5

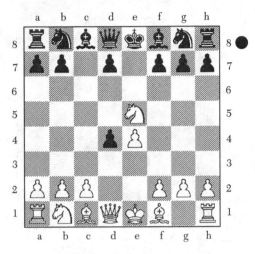

BLACK TO MOVE

Winning way: White's c5-knight is fodder after the forking **4. . . . Qa5+.** White cannot both disentangle himself from the check and save the knight with the same move.

How, what, and why: White blunders tactically by taking the pawn on e5, but it also doesn't make sense to first offer a pawn and then switch gears to take one. In the Sicilian Defense, Black has indirect sway over the fifth rank because his queen can often shift to a5 with check. So here e5 doesn't need direct protection. Rather than taking on e5, a more intelligent approach for White is to play 4. c2-c3, trying to open lines for attack. This tickling pawn push would soon prove the weakness of Black's two-square advance of the e-pawn.

RUY LOPEZ   **1.** e4 e5 **2.** Nf3 Nc6 **3.** Bb5 Nf6
            4. d3 Ne7 **5.** Nxe5 c6 **6.** Bc4

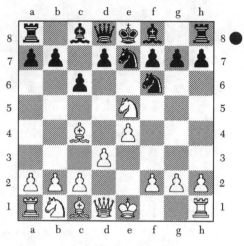

BLACK TO MOVE

Winning way: The winning move is 5. . . . c6. After the bishop retreats, Black has **6. . . . Qa5+** at his disposal. The fork to the enemy king and knight flypapers the knight on the next move.

How, what, and why: This is a devilish old trap. It looks as if Black has hung the e-pawn, so White takes it with the f3-knight. The satanic rejoinder is to move the c-pawn one square, jabbing at White's bishop and clearing the a5-d8 diagonal for the queen. The bishop naturally moves to safety, but this leaves the fifth rank vulnerable, and Black's queen usurps it. After White gets out of check, the queen enthralls White's arrant knave on e5. (On 6. Nc4, threatening a smothered mate on d6, Black triumphs by moving the d-pawn to d5, leaving White with two attacked minor pieces.)

25   Qa4+ is set up by d5

PONZIANI'S OPENING   **1.** e4   e5   **2.** Nf3   Nc6   **3.** c3   Nf6
                         4. d4   d6   **5.** Be2   Nxe4

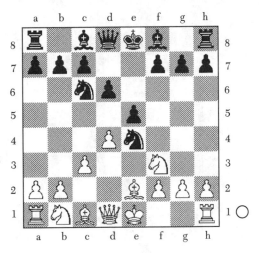

WHITE TO MOVE

Winning way: Material is plundered by **6. d5,** stabbing the knight at c6. If it moves to safety, White checks on a4 with the queen and adds the knight on e4 to his coffers.

How, what, and why: In the heart of the Amazon, on move five, it appears that Black's knight can take White's undefended king-pawn without consequence. But this is a jungle, and the pawn is indirectly ensnared in protection. The key lines of conjoining attack, the fourth rank and the a4-e8 diagonal, can be cleared by the immediate thrust d4-d5. After this, Black must lose one of his knights. In this game you must stay alert, for a sudden movement can render the terrain treacherous.

Qa5+ wins on g5

SLAV DEFENSE **1.** d4 d5 **2.** c4 c6 **3.** Nc3 Nf6
4. Bg5 Ne4 **5.** Nxe4 dxe4 **6.** e3

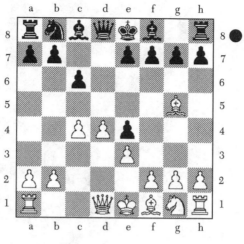

BLACK TO MOVE

Winning way: It's all over for the bishop after **1. . . . Qa5+.**
White can reply to the check in several ways, but none of them
rescue the piece on g5.

How, what, and why: The Slav Defense (2. . . . c6) opens the
a5-d8 diagonal to Black's queen, and the fifth rank also unblocks
after the recapture on e4. Nonetheless, a Black queen check on
a5 doesn't gather in the g5-bishop if the c1-h6 diagonal remains a
freeway, for the bishop can then be saved by blocking on d2 with
either queen or bishop. The criminal is White's sixth move, e2-
e3. This impedes the bishop's retreat and the White queen's
possible defense.

27 Qa5 leads to a winning discovery to g5

QUEEN'S GAMBIT DECLINED
   1. d4 d5 **2.** c4 e6
   3. Nc3 Nf6 **4.** Bg5 Nbd7
   5. Nf3 c6 **6.** e3 Qa5
   7. Qc2 Ne4 **8.** Bd3

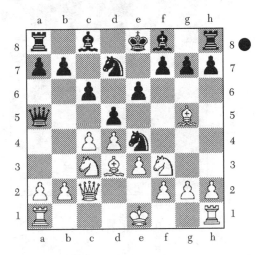

BLACK TO MOVE

Winning way: Black harvests a minor piece with **8. . . . Nxg5.** If White recaptures with the f3-knight, Black takes on c4 with the d5-pawn, and White must abandon either the bishop on d3 or the knight on g5.

How, what, and why: This is a variation of the Cambridge Springs line, which draws its name from the Pennsylvania town, the site of a famous 1904 tournament. With the Black queen on a5, White is susceptible to a fifth-rank discovery to g5. On move seven, White could safely exchange bishop for f6-knight. Another reprieve is offered by retreating the kingside knight to d2, breaking the pin on c3. But developing the bishop to d3 fails when Black swaps his way to a winning double attack.

28 Qa5+ wins on d5 after preventing Nc3

CATALAN OPENING   **1.** d4   d5   **2.** c4   c6   **3.** cxd5   cxd5
    4. g3   Bf5   **5.** Bg2   Nd7   **6.** Bxd5

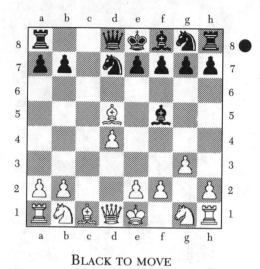

BLACK TO MOVE

Winning way: First Black removes the queen-knight, **6. . . . Bxb1.** After White takes back, Black acquires the d5-bishop by a forking queen check at a5. White can get out of check, but can't save the bishop.

How, what, and why: Since Black's fifth move, developing the knight to d7, obstructs the queen's defense of the d-pawn, White thinks he can take on d5 for free. White sees the queen check at a5, but concludes that it can be handled by blocking on c3 with the knight, securing the d5-bishop at the same time. What he overlooks is that the intended c3-blocker—and defender of d5—can be destroyed by simple capture, an in-between move, Bf5xb1, before it ever gets to c3. White then loses a piece. Either he doesn't take back on b1, and Black's b1-bishop retreats to safety, or he does take back and the queen check at a5 gains the d5-bishop.

NIMZOVICH DEFENSE   **1.** c4   Nc6   **2.** d4   d6
                 3. d5   Ne5   **4.** f4   Nxc4

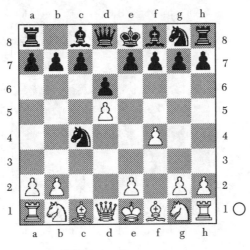

WHITE TO MOVE

Winning way: The Black knight is minced by **5. Qa4+**. This forks the Black king and knight. Only the king can be saved. Long live the king.

How, what, and why: Black gets greedy, and Black gets punished. Whenever knights surrender the center to enemy pawns in the opening, it's easy for the pawns to run roughshod. Here, White's pawns stampede Black's queen-knight, and the defender fails to grasp that White's c4-pawn doesn't need direct protection with White's queen armed for a forking check at a4. If you attack a pawn, and your opponent seems to ignore it, maybe he really hasn't.

30 Qa4+ wins on a6 after trading bishops

FRENCH DEFENSE **1.** e4 e6 **2.** d4 d5 **3.** e5 b6
4. c3 Ba6

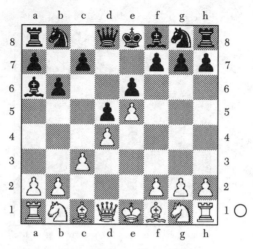

WHITE TO MOVE

Winning way: Start by trading bishops, **5. Bxa6.** After Black takes back, White forks the king and a6-knight by checking on a4 with the queen. The knight falls on the next move.

How, what, and why: In the French Defense, Black's "problem child" is the queen-bishop, which is often choked by the e6-pawn. If given the opportunity, Black would love to trade his queen-bishop for White's king-bishop. This explains Black's attempt to develop the bishop on the flank, to offer an exchange at a6. Note that to win on a6, White must first exchange and then check with the queen. If he checks with the queen first, before taking on a6, Black can save the day by blocking the check with his own queen. White must then respond to Black's threat to his queen, and lacks the time to capture the a6-bishop safely.

31   Qa4+ wins on a6 after sacrificing the exchange

QUEEN'S GAMBIT ACCEPTED   **1.** d4   d5   **2.** c4   dxc4
3. e4   b5   **4.** a4   c6
5. axb5   cxb5   **6.** b3   Ba6
7. bxc4   bxc4

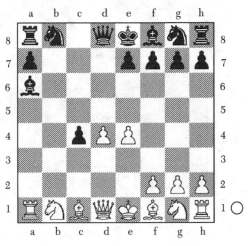

WHITE TO MOVE

Winning way: White's win begins with **8. Rxa6,** temporarily offering a rook for a bishop. After Black takes back on a6, White fires a queen salvo at a4 and wastes the a6-knight on the next move. White gets two pieces for a rook.

How, what, and why: Black veers from the principled path when he weakens the queenside by risky pawn advances, attempting to hold on to the gambit pawn. White's pawn moves, on the other hand, exploit this overextension. They open lines for attack, including the d1-a4 and a4-e8 diagonals, as well as the a-file. But an immediate queen check on move eight doesn't succeed. First a6 must be weakened by an exchange sac. Then the queen check at a4 grosses the knight at a6, resulting in White gaining two pieces for a rook.

32 Qa5+ wins on a7 after exchange sacrifice

SICILIAN DEFENSE   **1.** e4 c5   **2.** Nf3 d6   **3.** d4 cxd4
   4. Nxd4 e6   **5.** Be3 Nf6   **6.** f3 Be7
   7. Nb5 0-0   **8.** Nxa7

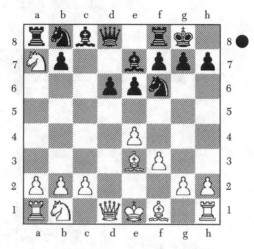

BLACK TO MOVE

Winning way: White pays for his pawn-grabbing when Black sacrifices the exchange, **8. . . . Rxa7!**. White's e3-bishop can capture the rook, but a forking queen check at a5 consigns the bishop to a less than noble fate.

How, what, and why: A sure way to lose in the opening is to invest time and resources to pick up a wing pawn at the expense of position and development. Here, White's bishop and knight zero in on Black's a-pawn, which is protected directly only by the a8-rook. But White misses that Black has a forking queen-check at a5, with the queen attacking backward along the a-file to a7. Black loses a rook but grabs the star-crossed bishop and knight. A good deal by chess standards.

33   Qa4 sets up discovery along the a4-e8 diagonal

SICILIAN DEFENSE   **1.** e4   c5   **2.** Nf3   Nc6   **3.** d4   cxd4
4. Nxd4   Nf6   **5.** Nc3   e5   **6.** Ndb5   d6
7. Nd5   Nxd5   **8.** exd5   Ne7   **9.** c4   a6

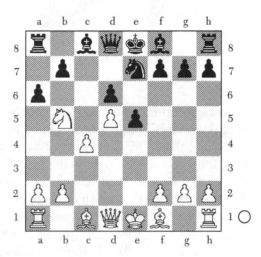

WHITE TO MOVE

Winning way: White wins by the unobtrusive **10. Qa4!**. Black is in trouble no matter what. If he takes the knight, White's queen removes the a8-rook. If he pins White's knight with the queen, Qd8-d7, the knight checks on c7, and suddenly Black's queen is frozen helplessly. Farewell, rook. That leaves 10. . . . Bd7, in which case White's knight takes on d6, smothering mate.

How, what, and why: In the end, Black makes the error of assuming that he has time to drive away White's advanced knight by advancing the a-pawn one square. But White's incisive queen move to a4 pins the a-pawn, and Black is tied up in knots. To save himself, Black must try a different ninth move, perhaps switching the knight to g6. This unclogs things and restores the f8-bishop's protection to d6.

♛

CHAPTER THREE

Qd5/Qd4

This is a small section of only eight examples, all of which revolve around a central queen move, queen to queen-five. In algebraic notation, that's Qd5 (queen to d5) for White and Qd4 (queen to d4) for Black. This is right in the board's middle. From d5 (Black's d4), the most typical stratagem is for the queen to deliver a multiple attack, often involving a check to the opposing king at f7 or g8 (f2 or g1 for Black's queen). Connection points include squares along the fifth rank (the fourth rank for Black) and the a8-h1 diagonal (for Black, the a1-h8 diagonal). In fact, the center is so fertile that it's not unusual to see a queen move there to attack three or four pieces in a kind of superfork.

34   Qd5 wins along a8-d5 diagonal

SICILIAN DEFENSE   **1.** e4   c5   **2.** Nf3   d6
                    3. d4   b6   **4.** dxc5   bxc5

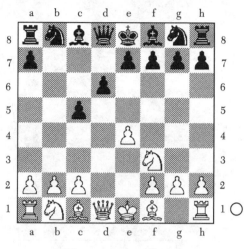

WHITE TO MOVE

Winning way: There's nothing to this one. The brazen **5. Qd5**, installing the queen at the central hub, wins at least a piece. In order to save the rook at a8, Black must jettison either a knight (Nb8-c6) or a bishop (Bc8-b7).

How, what, and why: Black misfires early when he fails to exchange the c-pawn for White's d-pawn, a primary objective in the Sicilian. By defending with the b-pawn, Black allows White to take on c5 with advantage. Either Black must take back with the d-pawn (d6xc5), permitting an unfavorable queen swap at d8, or abandon a piece by recapturing toward the center, b6xc5. Be wary of premature wing advances. They incur weaknesses and expose diagonal routes to the vulnerable corners.

SICILIAN DEFENSE   **1.** e4   c5   **2.** Nf3   Nc6   **3.** Bb5   d6
                4. b3   Nf6   **5.** Bxc6+   bxc6   **6.** e5   dxe5
                7. Nxe5

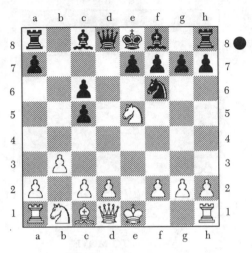

BLACK TO MOVE

Winning way: Black is victorious and White is vanquished by **7. . . . Qd4,** a two-timing fork to the a1-rook and the e5-knight. One of the two must leave River City.

How, what, and why: Although a queen in the middle of the board is often subject to a variety of attacks, the corollary is that a centralized queen is a powerful weapon, which can issue radial threats in all eight directions. Here, thanks to the early movement of White's b-pawn, the a1-e5 diagonal is quite ripe for queenly exploitation, especially after White errs with e4-e5, allowing an exchange that opens the d-file. What should White do about his attacked e-pawn? He should defend it, either with his queen-knight (6. Nb1-c3) or queen-pawn (6. d2-d3).

RUY LOPEZ   **1.** e4   e5   **2.** Nf3   Nc6   **3.** Bb5   f5
            4. d3   Bc5   **5.** 0-0   Nge7   **6.** Nc3   fxe4
            7. dxe4   0-0   **8.** Bxc6   Nxc6

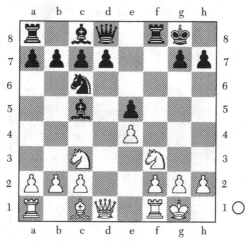

WHITE TO MOVE

Winning way: White hits two pieces—the opposing king and the dark-square bishop—and rebuffs Black's apparent attack by the squelching **9. Qd5+**. Next move, White collects the bishop.

How, what, and why: The eye-opener is the advance f7-f5. It's perfectly acceptable when Black plays it on move three, but moving the f-pawn in general entails a certain amount of baggage: namely, vulnerability along the a2-g8 diagonal once Black castles kingside. Put an unguarded Black bishop on c5, and a White queen check at d5 is bad news.

37   Qd4+ wins on c4 after clearing d4

BIRD'S OPENING   **1.** f4 d5 **2.** Nf3 c5 **3.** e3 Nc6
4. Be2 g6 **5.** 0-0 Bg7 **6.** Nc3 d4
7. exd4 Nxd4 **8.** Bc4

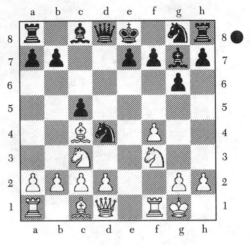

BLACK TO MOVE

Winning way: This is a two-mover. First Black trades knights, **8. . . . Nxf3+.** Assuming White takes back (what else?), Black follows with a queen fork at d4. White will have to get out of check, and Black pillages the c4-bishop next turn.

How, what, and why: The road signs are there: White is castled kingside, the f-pawn is moved, and White's light-square bishop occupies c4, undefended. Furthermore, the d-file is available to Black's queen, but d4 remains an obstacle, blocked by a Black knight. Eureka! Black exchanges the knight for an equivalent White piece with check. The check freezes the action, and Black has time to follow with another check, a forking one at d4. Voilà!

38   Qd5 threatens mate at f7 and the knight on e4

EVANS GAMBIT ACCEPTED   1. e4   e5   2. Nf3   Nc6
                       3. Bc4   Bc5   4. b4   Bxb4
                       5. c3   Bc5   6. 0-0   Nf6
                       7. d4   Bb6   8. dxe5   Nxe4

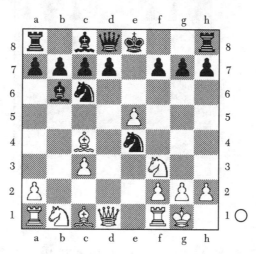

WHITE TO MOVE

Winning way: White has several ways to go, the strongest being **9. Qd5.** After Black rules out getting mated at f7, say by castling, White's queen freely captures Black's e4-knight.

How, what, and why: One potential drawback for Black is the unanchored e4-knight. Another nightmare is White's magisterial light-square bishop at c4, posted to support threats to f7. Both handicaps are linked in a losing complex by the centralizing invasion of White's queen to d5. Since the mate threat must be thwarted, the knight falls victim to the queen's universal radius of power.

39 Qd4 indirectly defends e5 in the Ruy Lopez

RUY LOPEZ   **1.** e4   e5   **2.** Nf3   Nc6   **3.** Bb5   Bc5
               4. d3   Nf6   **5.** Bxc6   dxc6   **6.** Nxe5

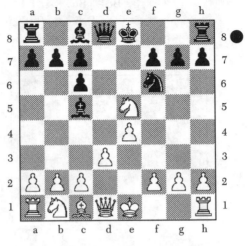

BLACK TO MOVE

Winning way: The best course of action is to give a double attack, **6. . . . Qd4.** This threatens both mate at f2 and the capture of the e5-knight. Regardless how White wards off mate, Black increases his worth (as a chessplayer).

How, what, and why: In the Ruy Lopez (1. e4 e5 2. Nf3 Nc6 3. Bb5), the usual way Black upholds his king-pawn, once White's bishop takes the c6-knight, is by d7xc6, taking away from the center. This opens the d-file, keeping in reserve the double attack Qd8-d4. The idea of this queen sortie is to hit the undefended points e5, e4, and f2. The f2-square counts when Black has a supporting bishop at c5 and when White has not yet castled. It also helps when the e5-knight cannot return to d3. Such is the storyline here.

BRUCE PANDOLFINI

40 Qd5 superforks a8, c5, e4, and f7

RUY LOPEZ   **1.** e4 e5 **2.** Nf3 Nc6 **3.** Bb5 a6
4. Ba4 Nf6 **5.** 0-0 b5 **6.** Bb3 Bc5
7. Nxe5 Nxe5 **8.** d4 Bd6 **9.** dxc5 Bxe5
10. f4 Bd6 **11.** e5 Bc5+ **12.** Kh1 Ne4

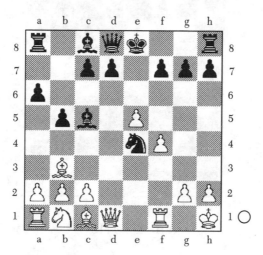

WHITE TO MOVE

Winning way: It seems like everything in the chessboard's physical universe is forked by **13. Qd5.** There's a mate threat at f7, the a8-rook and the e4-knight are hanging, and the c5-bishop is tenuous, held only by a free-falling knight. Something must go.

How, what, and why: Black's problems stem from the destruction of his center by White's fork trick, starting on move seven (White first sacs a knight on e5, then gets it back by a pawn fork on d4). Note how three critical lines of attack—the a8-h1 diagonal, the a2-g8 diagonal, and the d-file—all converge at d5, and White's queen vaults there at once. The radiant flex of a central queen!

DANISH GAMBIT   **1.** e4 e5 **2.** d4 exd4 **3.** c3 dxc3
                 4. Bc4 Bb4 **5.** bxc3 Ba5

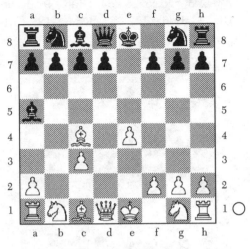

WHITE TO MOVE

Winning way: Double trouble it is after **6. Qd5.** Black can defend against the mate at f7, but only air holds up a5. The bishop is vaporized on the next move.

How, what, and why: Black's undoing begins with his fourth move, Bf8-b4. True, this threatens a discovery, c3×b2+, but it's easily frustrated by b2×c3. This forces Black to admit his mistake and retreat the b4-bishop. Unfortunately, a5 is not a haven. It's just as if the bishop has been sent below.

CHAPTER FOUR

♛

Qb3/Qb6

All thirteen illustrations in this section concern the movement of the queen to queen-knight-three (b3 for White, b6 for Black), with the queen typically moving from its original square. From queen-knight-three, the queen can do several things, including threatening the enemy king along the a2-g8 diagonal (the a7-g1 diagonal for Black) and attacking different opposing units on the b-file. A favorite motif is to form a battery of queen and bishop at c4 (c5 for Black) aimed at f7 (f2 for Black). When this is coupled with a direct threat to the enemy's undefended b-pawn (at b7 for White, b2 for Black) it tends to signal at least the gain of a pawn, if not much more.

42   Qb3 combines with Bc4 to win on f7

HUNGARIAN DEFENSE   **1.** e4   e5   **2.** Nf3   Nc6
                     3. Bc4   Be7   **4.** c3   d6   **5.** d4   h6

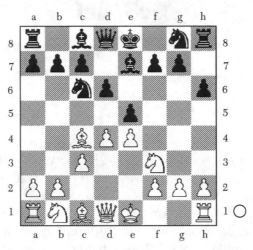

WHITE TO MOVE

Winning way: Black must cede a pawn after **6. Qb3,** for it can't be satisfactorily guarded (on Bc8-e6, White captures twice on e6). And if the f-pawn moves out of attack, White wins the g8-knight with a double strike along the a2-g8 diagonal.

How, what, and why: Black loses material, not for any reason in particular, but for a couple of them in combination. Black's fifth move is an outright error, which fails to deal with White's threat. Better is to develop the king-knight, followed by castling. Also note the position of Black's dark-square bishop at e7. It's okay in a vacuum, but here it impedes the queen's possible defense of f7. Chess abhors a vacuum. This way makes no sense.

43   Qb6 doubly attacks f2, winning a piece or mating at e3

FRENCH DEFENSE   **1.** e4   e6   **2.** d4   d5
3. Nd2   c5   **4.** dxc5   Bxc5
5. Ne2

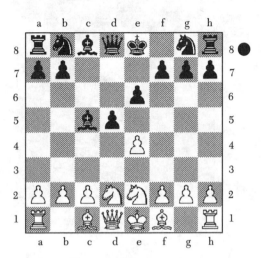

BLACK TO MOVE

Winning way: White is helpless after **5. . . . Qb6,** when mate can be averted only by sacrificing a knight, either Nd2-c4 or Ne2-d4. On other knight moves, the bishop enters on f2 and the queen mates at e3.

How, what, and why: This is similar to the previous problem in that the defending queen's access to the attacked square, here f2, is denied because of the obstruction of friendly forces. The knights at d2 and e2 are insurmountable hurdles, even for the White queen, which can't move to guard f2. This militates in favor of the active principle of knight development. Generally, it's better to position them on the third rank, where they have decent scope, rather than on the second rank, where they step on each other's hooves.

Paris Defense   **1.** e4   e5   **2.** Nf3   Nc6
                3. Bc4   d6   **4.** c3   Bg4   **5.** Qb3   Bxf3

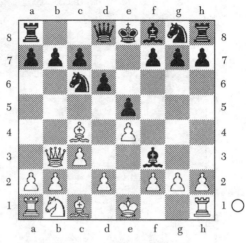

WHITE TO MOVE

Winning way: Taking the king-bishop-pawn with check does the magic. After **6. Bxf7+**, Black is mated by Qb3-e6, regardless of whether his king moves to d7 or e7.

How, what, and why: White's fifth move wins at least a pawn, for Black can't guard both b7 and f7 with the next move. An adequate defense is to play Qd8-d7. This protects f7 and also the c6-knight, so that if White's queen takes on b7, Black merely has to save his a8-rook (instead of having to worry about the c6-knight as well). But taking on f3 completely ignores White's mate threat. Probably Black assumes that White has to take back—but he doesn't. A tipoff to Black's difficulties is the early development of the queen-bishop. It leaves b7 undefended. Thus, when White's queen goes to b3, it's a double attack.

PHILIDOR DEFENSE   **1.** e4   e5   **2.** Nf3   d6
                    3. d4   Bg4   **4.** dxe5   Bxf3
                    5. Qxf3   dxe5   **6.** Bc4   Nf6

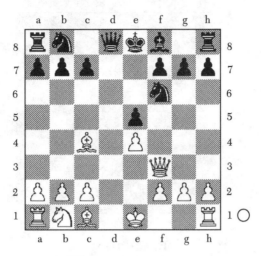

WHITE TO MOVE

Winning way: The b7-pawn disappears soon after **7. Qb3,** which forks b7 and f7. Black can save f7 and cope with the danger to his king by Qd8-e7. White then takes the b-pawn, tax-free.

How, what, and why: This example shows another route for the queen to reach b3 and double-attack heaven. Instead of going to b3 along the a4-d1 diagonal, it can also get there by shifting across the third rank. How does Black save his cornered a8-rook once White's queen captures on b7? By checking along the diagonal at b4, which forces a trade of queens. Still, after the queen trade, White is a pawn ahead with superior chances.

46   Qb6 wins on f2 because of Bxh3

Caro-Kann Defense   **1.** e4   c6   **2.** d3   d5   **3.** Nd2   e5
                      4. Be2   Bc5   **5.** c3   Qb6   **6.** Nh3

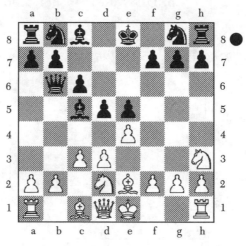

Black to move

Winning way: Black gets the edge by **6. . . . Bxh3,** removing the guard for f2. Once the defender takes back on h3, the f-pawn is taken with check, and for White it's downhill from there.

How, what, and why: Sometimes developing the knight to h3 to guard f2 works, but often it flops after the simple capture of the knight by the enemy queen-bishop. Usually, in order to keep the material balance, White will have to take back on h3, and f2 will be hanging again, as if it had never been protected by the h3-knight in the first place. Better for White is to bring out the king-knight to f3 on move five and to castle on move six, avoiding all this nonsense. As a rule, try to develop toward the center, placing your pieces harmoniously, without clash.

PHILIDOR DEFENSE   **1.** e4   e5   **2.** Nf3   d6
                   3. Bc4   Nd7   **4.** c3   Be7   **5.** d4   f6

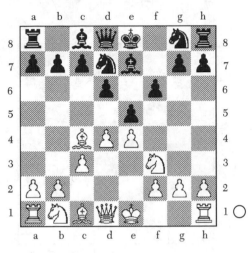

WHITE TO MOVE

Winning way: The piercing **6. Qb3** presents Black with a dilemma. Not only must he defend f7, he also has to wrestle with the threat to his g8-knight. And if the knight jumps to h6 to guard f7, White's queen-bishop removes it and a serious check at f7 is in the offing.

How, what, and why: Moving the pawn off the f7-square doesn't necessarily help. The pawn might not be vulnerable, but the square it used to be on can still be! And that's what's illustrated by doubling on the a2-g8 diagonal. Let's say Black plays 6. . . . Ng8-h6. After the attacker takes the h6-knight and follows with a check on f7, Black's king moves to f8. White's bishop retreats to h5, and mate is menaced at f7 by White's queen. It's time to try checkers.

GIUOCO PIANO | **1.** e4 | e5 | **2.** Nf3 | Nc6 | **3.** Bc4 | Bc5
| **4.** c3 | Qe7 | **5.** 0-0 | Bb6 | **6.** d4 | d6
| **7.** h3 | Bd7 | **8.** Qb3

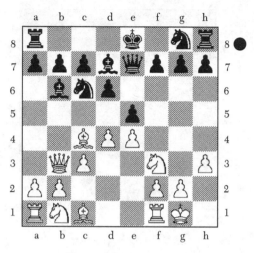

BLACK TO MOVE

Winning way: Refutation is in the air with **8. . . . Na5.** Black's knight forks White's queen and c4-bishop, and White can't save the queen and keep the bishop defended. The bishop dies an early death.

How, what, and why: White plays perfunctorily, delivering a superficial attack to f7, which is more than adequately upheld by Black's queen and king. Since Qd1-b3 threatens nothing, Black has time for a threat of his own, which emanates from the knight when it moves to a5. In some similar positions, the queen is able to move to a4, giving check and gaining time to save the day. But here a4 is guarded by the d7-bishop, while a5 is secured by the b6-bishop. White must give up the c4-bishop.

Na5 is refuted by Bxf7+ and Qa4

PARIS DEFENSE   **1.** e4 e5   **2.** Nf3 Nc6   **3.** Bc4 d6
               4. c3 h6   **5.** d4 Bg4   **6.** Qb3 Na5

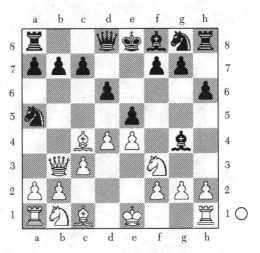

WHITE TO MOVE

Winning way: White wins with **7. Bxf7+**. Black moves his king to safety, and then White saves his queen by attacking the knight, say Qb3-a4. This counterthreat insures that White doesn't lose the f7-bishop for nothing. If Black takes it, White's queen takes the knight.

How, what, and why: Black's counteroffensive, forking with the knight at a5, hinges on a fallacy: the thought that after Black's king moves out of check, White will be unable to save his queen and still keep the f7-bishop defended. Black is right about the bishop, but wrong to assume that White doesn't have a strong reply. White's queen can move out of attack to menace Black's a5-knight, and this holds the position together. White remains a pawn ahead with Black's king in an exposed position.

KING'S INDIAN ATTACK   **1.** g3   d5   **2.** Bg2   e5   **3.** Nf3   Bd6
                              4. d3   Bg4   **5.** c4   Nf6
                              6. cxd5   Nxd5   **7.** Nc3   Nxc3
                              8. bxc3   0-0   **9.** 0-0   f5

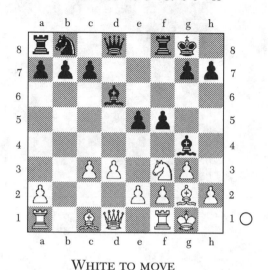

WHITE TO MOVE

Winning way: White gains a pawn by **10. Qb3+**. After Black disengages himself from the check, White's queen swallows the b7-pawn without entailment.

How, what, and why: If the queen-bishop is developed early, the b-pawn, which used to be defended by this bishop, is suddenly weakened, especially when the b-file is clear for rook and queen pressure. The situation worsens when Black is castled kingside and advances the f-pawn sharply, riskily opening the a2-g8 diagonal and exposing his own king. The connection point is b3. From there, White's queen can exploit Black's most sensitive spots at b7 and g8. If only Black's king were on another diagonal.

Qb6+ wins on b5

KING'S GAMBIT ACCEPTED   **1.** e4   e5   **2.** f4   exf4
                 3. Nf3   d5   **4.** exd5   Nf6
                 5. Bb5+   c6   **6.** dxc6   Nxc6
                 7. 0-0

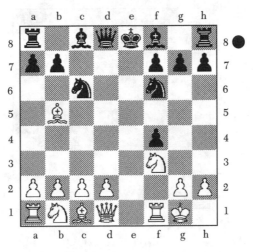

BLACK TO MOVE

Winning way: White's b5-bishop is a rotting carcass after **7. . . .** **Qb6+.** Whether White blocks the check by d2-d4 or moves his king to the corner, Black's queen swoops down on the bishop like a vulture.

How, what, and why: Castling is usually a wise move in the opening, but here it winds up placing the White king on the denuded a7-g1 diagonal. Then there's White's b5-bishop, which is just hanging out there by its lonesome. The queen shift to b6 hits both, wins one—the bishop. To avoid this loss, White shouldn't castle on move seven. Advancing the queen-pawn to d4, or taking the knight on c6 with check, or developing the queen-knight to c3, are more appropriate actions to undertake on the seventh move. They all avert the trap.

Qb3 skewers b4 and b7

ENGLISH OPENING **1.** c4 e5 **2.** Nc3 Nf6
3. Nf3 Nc6 **4.** g3 Bb4 **5.** Nd5 Nxd5
6. cxd5 e4 **7.** dxc6 exf3

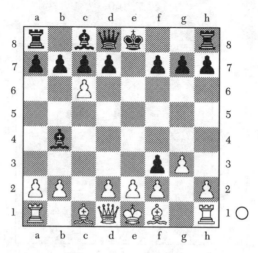

WHITE TO MOVE

Winning way: It's a skewer job, starting with **8. Qb3,** hitting the b4-bishop and the b7-pawn behind it. Even the craftiest defenses fail to hold both points satisfactorily, and Black must lose one of his bishops.

How, what, and why: If Black moves the b4-bishop to safety on move eight, White's pawn at c6 takes on b7, forking a8-rook and c8-bishop, backed up by White's queen. And if Black tries to keep the b4-bishop as a shield, defending it, say, with a7-a5, White merely drives the bishop away by a2-a3. From b3, White's queen, instead of attacking two points along two intersecting lines, assails two squares along the very same line (the b-file).

BRUCE PANDOLFINI

ENGLISH OPENING
1. c4 e5 **2.** g3 Nf6
3. Bg2 d5 **4.** cxd5 Nxd5 **5.** Nf3 f6
6. d3 Nc6 **7.** 0-0 Bb4 **8.** h3 0-0
9. Nc3 Nxc3 **10.** bxc3 Bxc3

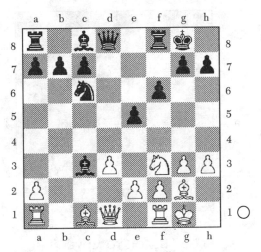

WHITE TO MOVE

Winning way: White capitalizes on Black's greed by **11. Qb3+.**
This is a fork, hitting the king at g8 and the bishop at c3. The
bishop at c3 will soon be no more, evermore.

How, what, and why: Black's fifth move is intended to
strengthen the e-pawn and the center, but actually it leaves the
a2-g8 line susceptible to enemy queen and bishop pressure.
Exchanging knights on c3 loses time, for it allows White to take
back, menacing the b4-bishop, which then must move to safety.
Capturing the c3-pawn is anything but safe, especially when
there's a lovely connection point at b3 for White's queen. A
better idea for Black on move nine would be to develop the
queen-bishop to e6, bolstering the a2-g8 diagonal.

54 Qb6 pins and wins the knight on d4

SICILIAN DEFENSE **1.** e4 c5 **2.** Nf3 d6
3. d4 cxd4 **4.** Nxd4 Nf6 **5.** Bd3 a6
6. Nd2 e6 **7.** f4 Be7 **8.** 0-0

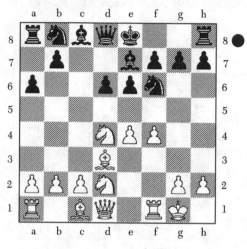

BLACK TO MOVE

Winning way: It's not hit and miss after **8. . . . Qb6.** It's hit and score on the d4-knight, which is pinned. White can protect his knight in several ways, but none of them stop Black from advancing the e-pawn on the next move, horsing it up to win a piece.

How, what, and why: Lots of things contribute to White's defeat. His bishop doesn't belong on d3, nor his knight on d2. They get in the way of the queen's natural defense of d4. Furthermore, White shouldn't castle on move eight with his f-pawn so advanced, for the a7-g1 diagonal is exposed to potential mayhem. A superior thought is to move the d2-knight to a more cooperative square (f3 or b3), defending d4 and clearing the c1-bishop's diagonal.

♛

CHAPTER FIVE

Qf3/Qf6

In this grouping, each of the eight examples hinges on developing the queen to king-bishop-three (f3 for White, f6 for Black). The double attacks that issue from this move are two-pronged: directed toward f7 (f2 for Black), which is often guarded solely by the opposing king, and to vulnerable points along the a8-f3 diagonal (the a1-f6 diagonal for Black), especially the cornered enemy queen-rook at a8 (a1 for the aggressive Black queen). Some of these sorties even produce mate, as in the famous Fried Liver Attack (example 58), popular with practically every young player. Supporting the queen's checkmating efforts may be a bishop positioned at c4 (c5 for Black) and/or a knight at g5 (for Black, g4).

Qf6 wins along the a1-f6 diagonal

BENONI DEFENSE   **1.** d4   c5   **2.** dxc5   e6   **3.** b4   a5
               4. c3   axb4   **5.** cxb4

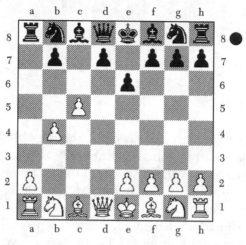

BLACK TO MOVE

Winning way: The job is done by **5. . . . Qf6,** and there's no way to avoid material loss. White must abandon either the rook at a1, the dark-square bishop at b2, or the queen-knight at c3.

How, what, and why: White's problems arise from the overreaching queenside pawn advances he makes at the expense of development. He commits himself to this strategy (b2-b4, c2-c3, and c3xb4) in order to try to hold onto the c5-pawn. The result is that the a1-f6 diagonal is riven open unblockably, and at least a minor piece is twiddled away.

QUEEN'S GAMBIT ACCEPTED   **1.** d4   d5   **2.** c4   dxc4
    3. Nf3   b5   **4.** a4   c6
    5. e3   Bd7   **6.** Ne5   e6
    7. axb5   cxb5

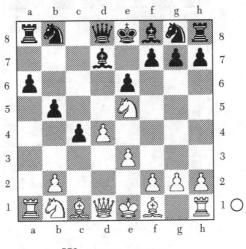

WHITE TO MOVE

Winning way: Double distress follows from **8. Qf3,** leaving both f7 and a8 in a sickly state. Black easily staves off mate, but the queen-rook might as well be antimatter. Ka-poof!

How, what, and why: Again it's a case of the loser losing because he advances the queenside pawns unwisely and precipitously, and again greed plays a role. The main reason Black takes on c4 is not to steal a pawn but to dissolve the center, perhaps getting some freedom of action and a somewhat easier game to play. So materialism goes against the grain of the position here. The linchpin is White's knight at e5. It's this piece that helps White issue the threat to f7, preventing Black from saving the a8-rook.

57 Qf3 sets up a Nf6+ discovery to d5-queen

VIENNA GAME **1.** e4 Nf6 **2.** Nc3 e5 **3.** Bc4 Nxe4
4. Nxe4 d5 **5.** Bxd5 Qxd5 **6.** Qf3 f5

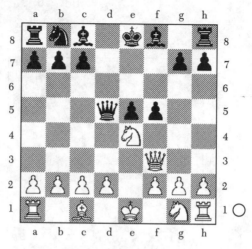

WHITE TO MOVE

Winning way: Kiss the queen goodbye after **7. Nf6+.** True, the knight can be taken for free, but so can Black's queen. You do the arithmetic.

How, what, and why: Black plays logically, breaking up White's center with a fork trick, starting with 3. . . . Nxe4. After White takes back, Black follows with d7-d5, which forks the bishop on c4 and the knight on e4. So Black's queen is brought to the center. This is not bad here, as long as Black stays awake and notices White's discovery threat after Qd1-f3. But Black doesn't see it, and White doesn't miss it.

TWO KNIGHTS DEFENSE   **1.** e4 e5 **2.** Nf3 Nc6
                        3. Bc4 Nf6 **4.** Ng5 d5
                        5. exd5 Nxd5 **6.** Nxf7 Kxf7
                        7. Qf3+ Ke6 **8.** Nc3 Nd4
                        9. Bxd5+ Ke7

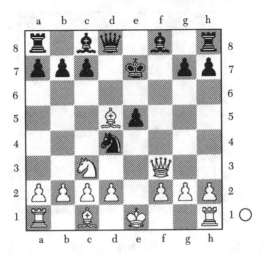

WHITE TO MOVE

Winning way: It's mate in two beginning with **10. Qf7+**. Black has no choice, being forced to move his king to d6, and White mates by checking with the knight at e4.

How, what, and why: White sacs a knight on move six to draw out Black's king, followed by an irksome queen check at f3. This coerces the enemy king to e6 to hold up the pinned d5-knight, which at that point is doubly attacked. White piles on the pressure, hitting the pinned target with his c3-knight. Black ignores White's threat to make one of his own. But White's check comes first, and when Black's king retreats to the wrong square (e7), a standard mate in two moves results.

Qf3 shifts to b3 and grabs b7

PHILIDOR DEFENSE   **1.** e4   e5   **2.** Nf3   d6   **3.** d4   Bg4
   4. dxe5   Bxf3   **5.** Qxf3   dxe5
   6. Bc4   Nf6   **7.** Qb3   Qd7
   8. Qxb7   Qc6

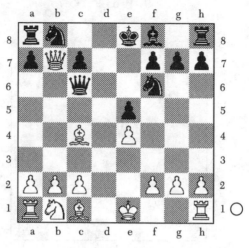

WHITE TO MOVE

Winning way: Black manages to save his rook, though he isn't so lucky with his queen, which is lost to the unnerving pin **9. Bb5.** Can't save them all.

How, what, and why: The square f3 is an excellent base for the queen to transfer the attack to the queenside. Once again, Black has to lose his b-pawn, but he doesn't have to surrender his queen (Qd8-d7-c6). On move seven, he could position his queen at e7 instead, as in example 45, which is the way the most famous chess game of all time began (Morphy vs. Count Isouard and the Duke of Brunswick, Paris, 1858). Morphy won that game, and many others. You can look it up.

QUEEN'S GAMBIT ACCEPTED   **1.** d4   d5   **2.** c4   e6   **3.** Nc3   c6
                             4. Bf4   dxc4 **5.** e3   b5
                             6. a4   Bb4   **7.** axb5 cxb5
                             8. Qf3   Qd5

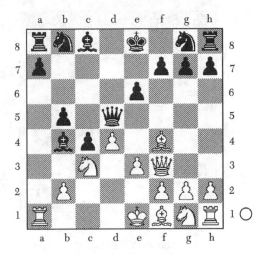

WHITE TO MOVE

Winning way: It's a mean, lowdown thing to do, but White exploits Black's specious play by **9. Qg3.** From g3, the queen hits at g7 and b8, the latter being attacked twice along the b8-f4 diagonal. However you look at it, it doesn't look good.

How, what, and why: Black thinks he's gotten away with the seizure of a White queenside pawn, but it's cost him time. White uses the time edge to develop the queen to f3, menacing the a8-rook, which is exposed along the a8-f3 diagonal. In order to save the rook, Black blocks the diagonal with his queen. But White's queen steps to the side to give a winning double attack to b8 and the unguarded g7-pawn (weakened when Black's dark-square bishop comes to b4).

61 Qf6 goes to d4 for diagonal mate to g1

THREE KNIGHTS GAME **1.** e4 e5 **2.** Nf3 Nc6 **3.** Nc3 Bc5
4. Nxe5 Bxf2+ **5.** Kxf2 Nxe5
6. d4 Qf6+ **7.** Kg1 Ng4 **8.** Qxg4

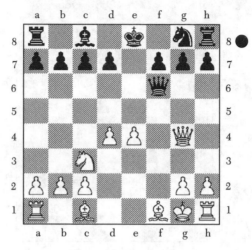

BLACK TO MOVE

Winning way: How quickly fortunes can change. Black gets rich
with **8. . . . Qxd4+**. White's only move is to block at e3 with the
bishop, and Black takes the bishop, mating.

How, what, and why: White initiates a fork trick (Nf3xe5) on
move four, and Black tries to regain his composure by sacrificing
his bishop on f2 with check, to take away White's right to castle.
White gets the center, however, and might do well enough if he
resists Black's knight on g4. He doesn't, the d-pawn falls with
check, and mate along the b6-g1 diagonal cannot be headed
off—a queenly channel of ingress to White's king.

62   Qf3 to b3 gives a criss-cross mate

CARO-KANN DEFENSE   **1.** e4   c6   **2.** d4   d5   **3.** Nc3   dxe4
4. Nxe4   Nf6   **5.** Nxf6+   exf6
6. Bc4   Be7   **7.** Qh5   0-0   **8.** Ne2   g6
9. Qf3   Nd7   **10.** Bh6   Re8
11. Bxf7+   Kxf7

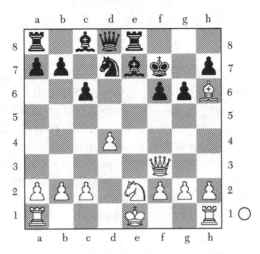

WHITE TO MOVE

Winning way: It's mate by **12. Qb3#.** The diagonal check comes from far away, but it's very effective. And the dark squares around the Black king? They're eaten up by the h6-bishop.

How, what, and why: White employs his queen most profitably, invading on h5 and inducing a pawn weakness, g7-g6. White stays flexible, retreating the queen to f3 and retaining options across and up and down. Black stumbles further, blocking d7 with a knight, which prevents the queen-bishop from deploying to e6. One White bishop assumes control over the dark squares (Bc1-h6) and the other is sacrificed at f7, only to be replaced diagonally by the ubiquitous queen.

♛

Queen Gallimaufry

The twelve paradigms in Chapter Six refer to a number of different winning queen moves, including ones to several points along the g-file, to the squares d4 and e4, and a few other odds and ends. While these tactics tend to occur a little less often than the previous groups, each is relevant and should assume a valued place in a student's attacking repertoire. The chief target square in the section is g7 (g2 for Black). As the examples demonstrate, the square can come under fire whether the defender is castled or not.

ITALIAN GAME   **1.** e4   e5   **2.** Nf3   Nc6   **3.** Bc4   Nd4
               4. Nxe5   Qg5   **5.** Nxf7   Qxg2
               6. Nxh8   Qxe4+   **7.** Kf1

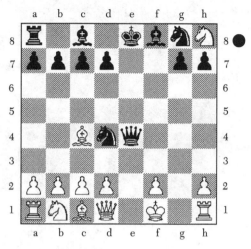

BLACK TO MOVE

Winning way: Black's imperial queen puts the finishing touch on the position with **7.... Qxh1#.** Unless the rules have changed, this is mate.

How, what, and why: The problems for White begin on move four, with the apprehension of the e-pawn. This enables Black's queen to issue a typical double attack at g5, thwacking at the brazen knight as well as the undefended g2-pawn. White thinks he has the solution, taking on f7, forking the queen on g5 and the rook on h8. Black's bludgeoning capture at g2, however, is the brutal answer, and suddenly White's position is in tatters. Sure, White chomps a rook, but Black delivers an ultimatum when his queen takes on e4 with check. Either White surrenders his queen (7. Qxc2) or is mated. Temerity prevails (7. Kf1), termination ensues (7.... Qxh1#).

SICILIAN DEFENSE **1.** e4 c5 **2.** Nf3 Nc6 **3.** Nc3 g6
4. Bb5 Nd4 **5.** Nxd4 exd4 **6.** Nd5 e6
7. Nf4

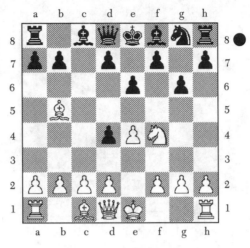

BLACK TO MOVE

Winning way: White's lead in development actually backfires after the forking sally **7. . . . Qg5.** Two pieces are assailed, the knight at f4 and the bishop at b5, and only one can be salvaged.

How, what, and why: In the Sicilian Defense, it's not uncommon for Black to play several early pawn moves and for White to mobilize his pieces sooner. But having more pieces out doesn't guarantee superior placement. After 6. Nd5, White has aggressively positioned minor pieces, but they are surrounded by menacing pawns, so that the counter e7-e6 forces the advanced knight to accept an infelicitous retreat. The move Qd8-g5 is usually played to harass g2. Here it reaps an unexpected harvest, the fork of b5 and f4, and White must drop a piece.

Qg4+ defends e4

SICILIAN DEFENSE
1. e4 c5 **2.** Nf3 d6 **3.** Bb5+ Bd7
4. Bxd7+ Nxd7 **5.** 0-0 Qc7
6. d4 cxd4 **7.** Nxd4 0-0-0 **8.** Be3 a6
9. Nb3 Ndf6 **10.** a4 Nxe4

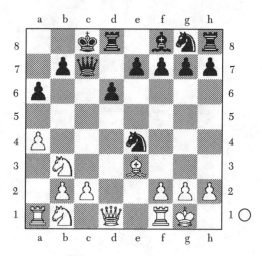

WHITE TO MOVE

Winning way: Black thinks he is pilfering a pawn, but White makes him pay for this plunder by **11. Qg4+.** No matter how Black addresses the check, the e4-knight is lost.

How, what, and why: One way to stop the sharp rejoinder Qd1-g4 is to maintain a knight at f6. This positioning guards the kingside and stands sentinel over g4. Typically, if the f6-knight captures on e4, the counter Qd1-g4 will threaten e4 and g7. The square g7 is not important here, for g7 is still upheld. But by castling queenside, Black has stationed his king on the exposed c8-h3 diagonal. Thus, after the knight captures on e4, White's queen can zoom to g4, checking the king, stopping the action, and dispatching the e4-knight to the junk heap.

66 Qg4 threatens mate at g7 and a discovery

RUY LOPEZ **1.** e4 e5 **2.** Nf3 Nc6 **3.** Bb5 Bc5 **4.** d3 d6
5. 0-0 Bg4 **6.** Nbd2 Ne7 **7.** Bxc6+ Nxc6
8. h3 Bxf3 **9.** Nxf3 Qd7 **10.** Nh4 0-0
11. Nf5 d5

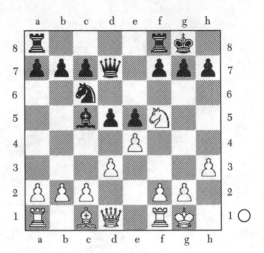

WHITE TO MOVE

Winning way: The killer is **12. Qg4.** This threatens mate at g7. Regardless how Black defends, whether by moving the g-pawn or the f-pawn, White's knight checks on h6, uncovering a triumphant attack from White's queen to Black's.

How, what, and why: After castling kingside, it's natural for Black to assume that g7 is secure. But White's knight at f5 changes things. It overlooks g7 and screens Black's queen from defense of g4. So White's queen can move to g4 without fear of being captured. Worse, the f5-knight allows White to position his queen with a double threat to g7 and d7 for which there is no satisfactory defense. The problem for Black is his eleventh move, d6-d5. Safer is to offer a trade of knights (Nc6-e7 or Nc6-d4) or to move the king to the corner (Kg8-h8), making sure that White's knight isn't able to move and also give check.

67   Qg5 threatens mate at g2 and Nf3+

RUY LOPEZ   **1.** e4   e5   **2.** Nf3   Nc6   **3.** Bb5   Nge7
4. d4   exd4   **5.** Nxd4   Ng6   **6.** 0-0   Bc5
7. Be3   Bxd4   **8.** Bxd4   Nh4   **9.** Nc3   Nxd4
10. Qxd4

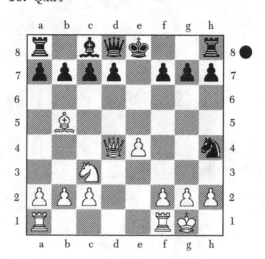

BLACK TO MOVE

Winning way: Victory is achieved by **10. . . . Qg5.** This threatens mate at g2. White can defend against the mate by moving the g-pawn one square (g2-g3), but that allows a knight check at f3, winning White's queen.

How, what, and why: When a knight and the queen combine to attack g2, typically the knight contributes its part from f4. Yet the threat can have the same potency with the knight on h4, so that instead of h3 coming under the knight's fire, it's f3 that's additionally hit. Note that Black would have the same winning fork even if White's g-pawn were back on g2, in that Black's queen would pin the pawn to the g-file, preventing it from capturing on f3. While 10. . . . Qd8-g5 is crushing, the actual winning idea comes about a move earlier, when Black exchanges on d4, drawing White's queen onto a forkable square (d4).

FRENCH DEFENSE   **1.** e4 e6 **2.** d4 d5 **3.** Nc3 dxe4
4. Nxe4 Nd7 **5.** Nf3 Ngf6
6. Nxf6+ Nxf6 **7.** Bd3 Be7
8. Bg5 0-0 **9.** Qe2 b6

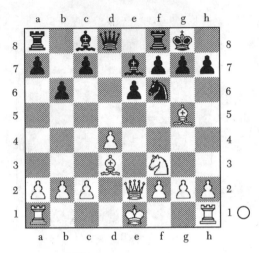

WHITE TO MOVE

Winning way: White gives Black the old one-two. First he captures a key defensive piece, **10. Bxf6.** After Black takes back, White follows with a queen fork at e4, menacing mate at h7 and the rook in the corner. The king will be saved, the rook abandoned, just like in real life.

How, what, and why: Black's troubled piece in the French Defense is the light-square bishop, which early on is blocked by the e6-pawn. In trying to find activity for this piece, Black moves his b-pawn (b7-b6), hoping to fianchetto at b7. But this advance weakens the a8-e4 diagonal. White can't capitalize on this breach with Black's f6-knight guarding e4, which explains the exchange initiated on move ten (Bg5xf6), removing the defender. To maintain the material balance, Black must take back, and White's queen blisters from e4.

Qd4 hits b4 and g7

GORING GAMBIT   **1.** e4 e5 **2.** d4 exd4 **3.** c3 dxc3
               4. Nxc3 Bb4 **5.** Qd4 Nc6 **6.** Qxg7 Qf6
               7. Bh6 d6

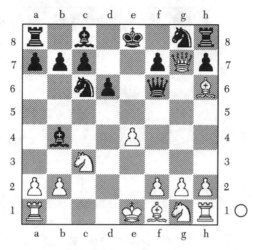

WHITE TO MOVE

Winning way: White conquers with the uncomplicated ex-change **8. Qxf6.** After the knight takes back on f6, White's bishop succeeds in forking knight and rook by Bh6-g7.

How, what, and why: Black commits the error of thinking that his g-pawn is expendable because of the time White loses in moving his queen twice. The move 7. Bc1-h6 comes as a sur-prise, since Black has two pieces (the queen and knight) guard-ing h6. But each of these fulfills a necessary function: the queen props up h8 and the knight protects the queen. If either one takes on h6, the system breaks down and something goes. Mean-while, if Black does essentially nothing, he is victimized by an exchange on f6 and a fork on g7. Some days you can't make a living.

SICILIAN DEFENSE   **1.** e4   c5   **2.** b4   cxb4   **3.** a3   d5
                     4. exd5   Qxd5   **5.** axb4

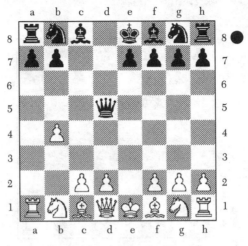

BLACK TO MOVE

Winning way: Although White regains his sacrificed pawn, Black makes him pay dearly with **5. . . . Qe5+.** How White gets out of check is irrelevant, for his a1-rook is downed next move, 6. . . . Qxa1.

How, what, and why: The usual idea behind White's second move, b2-b4, offering the b-pawn as a gambit, is to lure Black's c5-pawn out of the center, allowing White to follow with a two-square push of the d-pawn. But White delays the d-pawn's advance in order to open more lines on the queenside by moving the a-pawn. Black correctly counters in the center, moving out his d-pawn, knowing that White's queen-knight is unable to develop to c3, thanks to the b4-pawn. So White takes the b4-pawn, 5. a3xb4, but before he can develop his knight to attack Black's queen, Her Majesty gives a telling check at e5, which forks the rook at a1 and wins it.

71   Qg6 wins because f7 is pinned

VIENNA GAME   **1.** e4 e5   **2.** Nc3 Nf6   **3.** Bc4 Nxe4
4. Qh5 Nd6   **5.** Bb3 Be7   **6.** Nf3 0-0
7. h4 Nc6   **8.** Ng5 h6   **9.** Nd5 Nd4
10. Nxe7+   Qxe7

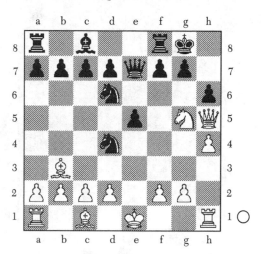

WHITE TO MOVE

Winning way: White fulfills his ambitions by **11. Qg6!**, threatening mate at h7. If the defender takes White's knight, 11. . . . hxg5, White retakes, 12. hxg5, opening the h-file for the rook, and Black can't stop the same threat at h7.

How, what, and why: Black tries to safeguard his king but actually castles into a gathering storm. Problems are manifest after White's eighth move, with mate threatened at h7. Black doesn't take the knight (8. . . . Be7xg5), to avoid opening the h-file (9. h5xg6). So he must move his h-pawn (8. . . . h7-h6), and both sides wind up centralizing a knight (9. Nd5 Nd4): White's for attack, Black's for defense, to eliminate the b3-bishop. But White trades on e7 and invades with the queen, again thinking mate. This time, Black is a move short of mustering a defense.

72 Qg3 induces h3xg4, allowing Qh4 mate

SCOTCH GAME   **1.** e4   e5   **2.** Nf3   Nc6   **3.** d4   exd4
4. Nxd4   Nf6   **5.** Nc3   Bb4   **6.** Nxc6   bxc6
7. Bd3   0-0   **8.** 0-0   d5   **9.** e5   Ng4
10. f4   Qh4   **11.** h3   Bc5+   **12.** Kh1

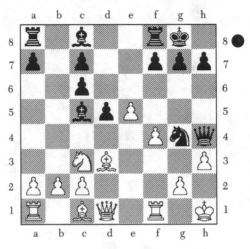

BLACK TO MOVE

Winning way: Black consummates his attack with the intrusive
12. . . . Qg3!, proposing to mate at h2. Unless White cedes his
queen, 13. Qd1xg4 Bc8xg4, he must take the knight with his
rook-pawn, permitting a queen-mate at h4.

How, what, and why: White gets into hardship over his e-pawn.
Instead of trading it off on move nine, or defending it on move
ten with his queen-bishop, he chooses to protect it with his
f-pawn. This opens the a7-g1 diagonal for Black's bishop. After
Black forces a weakness at g3 (10. . . . Qh4 11. h3), the bishop
checks at c5, driving White's king to the corner. The invasion of
the queen to g3 is a standard tactic. It forces open the h-file to
stop the mate at h2 (13. h3xg4), and the queen then goes back to
where it was on h4. But this time, with White's h-pawn gone and
his king unsheltered, it's mate.

TWO KNIGHTS DEFENSE   **1.** e4   e5   **2.** Nf3   Nc6
                         3. Bc4   Nf6 **4.** d4   exd4
                         5. 0-0   d5   **6.** exd5 Na5

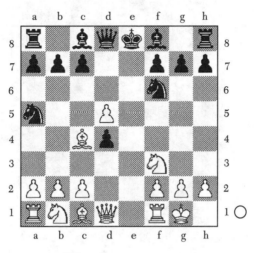

WHITE TO MOVE

Winning way: Black's knight attacks his opponent's bishop, but it's the knight that's really in trouble after **7. Qe1+.** Black must untangle himself from check and White then gloms onto the knight, Qe1xa5.

How, what, and why: Black makes several mistakes. First, he willingly allows the center to open with his king still on its original square by exchanging d-pawn for e-pawn. Then he moves the queen-knight a second time, foolishly placing it on a5, where it has reduced scope. The surprise is White's queen check from e1. Usually the rook gives this check, but by employing the queen, White issues a deadly fork and punishes Black's carelessness.

RETI'S OPENING   **1.** Nf3   c5   **2.** e3   Nc6   **3.** Bb5   d5
4. 0-0   e6   **5.** Bxc6+   bxc6   **6.** Ne5   Nf6
7. Nxc6

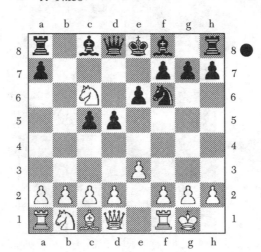

BLACK TO MOVE

Winning way: White has won a pawn, but he's about to lose a knight after **7. . . . Qc7.** The horse is threatened and it has no safe retreat. Just try to protect it. You can't!

How, what, and why: White should realize that something is up when he attacks Black's doubled c6-pawn and his opponent seemingly ignores the threat by developing his king-knight. Taking the pawn on c6 looks good initially, because it also gains time by attacking Black's queen. But Black can save his queen and, in the process, counterattack the knight while also usurping all the knight's escape squares. The knight is simply trapped and done for after 7. . . . Qc7. In chess, you shouldn't go in if you can't get out.

CHAPTER SEVEN

Bxf7/Bxf2 and Nxe5/Nxe4

With this chapter, we leave the world of queens and bring on the minor pieces (bishops and knights). The twenty-three examples in this section feature attacks along the a2-f7 diagonal (the a7-f2 diagonal for Black), especially directed at f7 (for Black, f2), and knight captures on e5 (e4 for Black) and/or incursions to g5 (g4) discovering attacks along the d1-h5 diagonal (the d8-h4 diagonal for Black). Among the themes is the well-known Legal's Mate, in which the queen is sacrificed to bring about checkmate with several minor pieces in different combinations and settings. It's a long chapter, with many related but slightly different problems, so play through it carefully.

CENTER COUNTER DEFENSE   **1.** e4   d5   **2.** Nc3   dxe4
                          3. Nxe4   e5   **4.** Bc4   Nf6

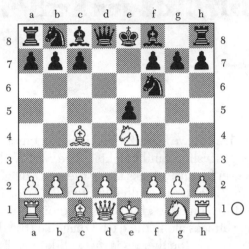

WHITE TO MOVE

Winning way: White reminds Black how sensitive f7 is with **5. Ng5.** The only hope is to block out the c4-bishop by 5. . . . Nf6-d5, which loses at least a pawn to 6. Qf3! Qxg5 7. Bxd5, and Black can't hold up b7 and f7 concurrently.

How, what, and why: Black might have essayed the alternative defense 5. . . . Bc8-e6, which stumbles into a bust-up trade, 6. Ng5xe6 f7xe6, and a forking queen check at h5, winning the forward e-pawn. Whenever the king-bishop zeroes in on f7 and the defender is uncastled, he must be vigilant against a knight invasion to g5. Thus Black's fourth move, the normally natural Ng8-f6, is actually a mistake. Sagacity prevails with a different fourth move, Bf8-e7. This delays developing the king-knight for one move, but it guards g5 and nurtures castling, an excellent way to protect a beleaguered f7-square.

Bc5 pins queen to king

SICILIAN DEFENSE **1.** e4 c5 **2.** Nf3 Nc6 **3.** d4 cxd4
4. Nxd4 e6 **5.** Be2 a6 **6.** 0-0 Qc7
7. f4

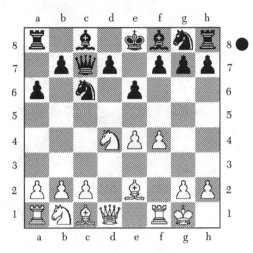

BLACK TO MOVE

Winning way: White thinks his position is all boarded up, but his last move, weakening the a7-g1 diagonal, was premature. Black purloins a piece by **7. . . . Nxd4,** when taking back loses the queen to a nailing pin at c5 by the bishop.

How, what, and why: The advance of the f-pawn in the Sicilian is a typical move for White, but it often requires preparation. Three common ways to ready the advance are: (a) moving the knight from d4, say to b3, so that it can't be pinned; (b) shifting the king to the corner, off the a7-g1 line, so that there's nothing to pin the d4-knight to; or (c) developing the queen-bishop to e3, strengthening the diagonal against pinning assailants. White does none of these and suffers the consequences.

QUEEN'S GAMBIT ACCEPTED   **1.** d4   d5   **2.** c4   dxc4
          3. e3   g6   **4.** Bxc4   b6
          5. Ne2   Bb7   **6.** 0-0   Qd6
          7. Nbc3   a6   **8.** a3   Qc6

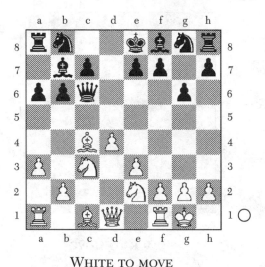

WHITE TO MOVE

Winning way: Black has two threats, to mate at g2 and to capture at c4 free. But it's White's turn, and just like the road not taken, this makes all the difference. After **9. Bd5,** Black must flee with his queen, and the b7-bishop is ravaged by the d5-bishop.

How, what, and why: Black determines that he has a clever trap, lining up on the a8-g2 diagonal to threaten mate, combined with a swipe at the c4-bishop. But by placing his queen on c6 in front of his own bishop, he actually signs over control of the long diagonal to White, who has two pieces guarding d5. So White's bishop can then move to d5, saving itself and bogging the mating line, with a gain of time by counterattacking the queen. The queen must move to safety, relinquishing its hold on the hapless b7-bishop, which is then expropriated.

RUY LOPEZ   **1.** e4 e5 **2.** Nf3 Nc6 **3.** Bb5 a6
4. Ba4 Nf6 **5.** 0-0 d6 **6.** c3 b5
7. Bb3 Nxe4

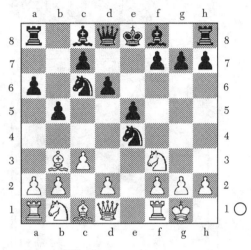

WHITE TO MOVE

Winning way: Black's rapacious grab of e4 leaves him vulnerable to the two-pronged counter **8. Bd5.** Forked, the velociraptor must fight for survival without further support from at least one of his knights. White wins a piece.

How, what, and why: In the Ruy Lopez, Black keeps a watchful eye on White's e4-pawn, hoping to have the opportunity to take it. But if he's going to do so, better timing requires capturing it on move five, before White's light-square bishop has been driven to b3 by the advance b7-b5. The drawback to this last push is that it weakens the a8-e4 diagonal, and especially c6. So White sets a trap. Instead of protecting the e-pawn with his f1-rook on move seven, he lets it "hang" for one move more, hoping Black takes it. Black does, and the harvest is a chess education.

79   Bxd5+ regains the Fried Liver piece

TWO KNIGHTS DEFENSE   **1.** e4   e5   **2.** Nf3   Nc6
3. Bc4   Nf6   **4.** Ng5   d5
5. exd5   Nxd5   **6.** Nxf7   Kxf7
7. Qf3+   Ke6   **8.** Nc3   Nd4
9. Bxd5+   Ke7

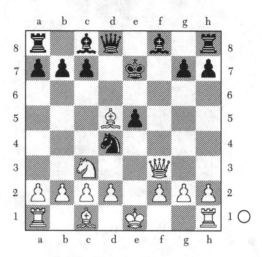

WHITE TO MOVE

Winning way: White's queen is beset with knight trauma, but the really traumatic stuff is about to happen to Black, who gets mated after **10. Qf7+.** Black must play his king to d6, where it encounters a knightmarish check from e4. That's mate.

How, what, and why: White's knight sacrifice on f7 constitutes the Fegatello, or Fried Liver, Attack. Supposedly, an Italian master played it centuries ago while eating fried liver. It usually gives Black indigestion, especially when he ignores defense and tries to gorge further with the queen-hungry 8. . . . Nc6-d4. Healthier is to sop up the acid with a defensive eighth move, either Nc6-e7 or Nc6-b4. But some players can't stomach defense.

PHILIDOR DEFENSE   **1.** e4   e5   **2.** Nf3   d6   **3.** d4   Bg4
                   4. dxe5   Bxf3   **5.** Qxf3   dxe5
                   6. Bc4   Nf6   **7.** Qb3   b6

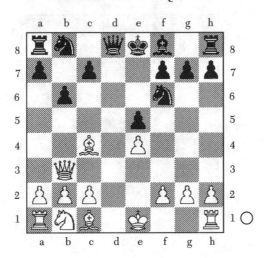

WHITE TO MOVE

Winning way: Black is disposed of by **8. Bxf7+.** The defender has two choices. He can move his king to either d7 or e7 and get mated at e6 by White's queen. Or he can resign. As Woody Allen says, let us hope he chooses wisely.

How, what, and why: When White transfers his queen to b3, he promulgates two threats: one to b7, the other to f7. Black's seventh move, b7-b6, nullifies the attack to b7, but it does nothing to neutralize the battery of queen and bishop directed toward f7. A seventh-move improvement is to deploy Black's queen at e7, preventing mate. Then if White takes on b7, Black can force a queen trade by checking on b4. If Black wishes to avoid this, he should do something other than developing the queen-bishop on move three. Either taking on d4 or putting the queen-knight at d7 work fine.

PARIS DEFENSE   **1.** e4   e5   **2.** Nf3   Nc6   **3.** Bc4   d6
                4. c3   h6   **5.** d4   Nf6   **6.** dxe5   Nxe4

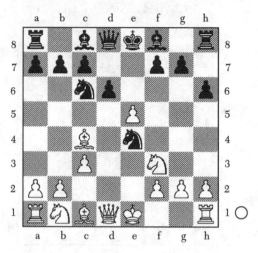

WHITE TO MOVE

Winning way: White wins by the temporary sacrifice **7. Bxf7+**, which forces Black's king to move. After the bishop is captured, White's queen checks at d5, picking up the knight at e4. Overall, White gains a pawn and Black loses the right to castle.

How, what, and why: Once again d5 is at the core of activity, and White is able to occupy this square to exert influence along intersecting diagonals. White draws out the Black king by sacrificing the bishop along the a2-g8 diagonal, and White's follow-up queen check at d5 exploits the a8-h1 diagonal to assault the e4-knight. Sometimes the crosscutting tactic works by moving the queen to d5 directly (the so-called slow way), without first sacrificing the bishop on f7 (the fast way). But here 7. Qd1-d5 fails to 7. . . . Bc8-e6. If White's queen then takes the e4-knight, Black recoups the piece by a pawn fork at d5.

BISHOP'S OPENING   **1.** e4 e5 **2.** Bc4 Bc5 **3.** Qe2 c6

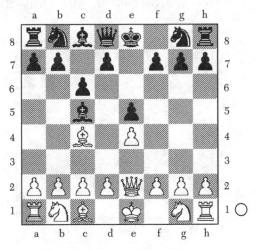

WHITE TO MOVE

Winning way: Black fails to discern the cosmic significance of White's early queen move. His universe is expanded by **4. Bxf7+.** After the king takes the bishop, White's queen checks at c4, regaining the piece plus a pawn.

How, what, and why: This example comes prior to the big-bang days of chess, when folks were not used to the powers of the pieces. Change Black's third move, developing the king-knight to f6 instead, and a new cosmology emerges. If on move three Black plays Ng8-f6, sacrificing the bishop on f7 leads to 4. . . . Kxf7 5. Qc4+ d5 6. Qxc5 Nxe4. Here, material is even, and though the defender's king has moved, it's not endangered, and Black owns the center of the Milky Way.

83　Bxf7+ deflects e8 from defense of d8

SICILIAN DEFENSE　**1.** e4　c5　**2.** d4　cxd4　**3.** c3　dxc3
　　　　　　　　　4. Nxc3　d6　**5.** Bc4　Nf6　**6.** e5　dxe5

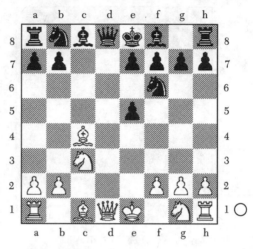

WHITE TO MOVE

Winning way: Black's queen is atomized by **7. Bxf7+!.** The bishop must be taken by the king, leaving Black's queen unguarded. With the d-file clear, a thankful White queen beams to d8 and captures its prize.

How, what, and why: Black's king is overloaded. It's tied to guarding the queen at d8 and the pawn at f7. If the king is forced to respond to a threat on one of these squares, suddenly it will be out of position to reply to an attack on the other. White's bishop at c4 is the crux. By sacrificing it on f7, White deflects Black's king away from the queen. A common mistake in similar open d-file situations is to trade queens first (Qd1xd8+) and then capture on f7 (Bc4xf7), but that wins only a pawn.

Sicilian Defense   **1.** e4   c5   **2.** Nf3   d6   **3.** d4   cxd4
4. Nxd4   Nf6   **5.** Nc3   g6   **6.** f4   Bg7
7. e5   dxe5   **8.** fxe5   Ng4   **9.** Bb5+   Kf8

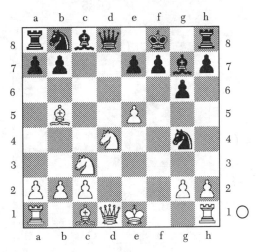

WHITE TO MOVE

Winning way: Black loses the right to castle, then the queen,
and perhaps his mind after **10. Ne6+.** It doesn't matter how the
check is dealt with; White's queen devours Black's on move
eleven.

How, what, and why: Black is already in trouble when White
fires a bishop check on move nine. If he answers by blocking at
d7 with the bishop, he puts his own bishop in a pin, and White's
queen can take the knight on g4 for nothing. The best try is 9. . . .
Nc6, which is countered by 10. Nxc6 Qxd1+ 11. Kxd1! Nf2+ 12.
Ke2 Nxh1 13. Nd4+, when White will follow with Bc1-f4 and
Ra1xh1. White gets two pieces for a rook, but the game is still a
fight. But sidling the king to f8 on move nine is a loser. White
simply throws the knight away with check, clearing the d-file to
gain Black's queen.

85   Bb4+ uncovers an attack on the d-file

QUEEN'S GAMBIT DECLINED   **1.** d4   d5   **2.** c4   e6   **3.** Nf3   c5
                                     4. cxd5   exd5   **5.** e3   Bd6
                                       6. Be2   cxd4   **7.** Qxd4   Nc6
                                       8. Qxd5

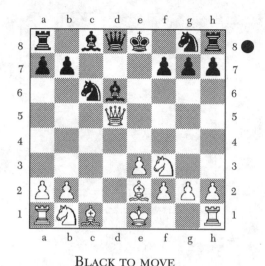

BLACK TO MOVE

Winning way: The White queen is undefended and vincible in the middle. But nothing attacks it until **8. . . . Bb4+.** That's a check to the king and a discovery to the queen. White can end the check, but he can't save the queen.

How, what, and why: The most troubling discoveries are those that come suddenly, springing forth in full checking flower. The check essentially freezes the action, denying the defender the chance to play any move other than one that ends check. Here it seems that by playing the knight to c3, White could actually block Black's check and guard his queen at the same time. However, this block (9. Nb1-c3) doesn't work. Black can take the knight with check (9. . . . Bb4xc3+) and then capture the queen (10. . . . Qd8xd5), or he can simply capture the queen at once (9. . . . Qd8xd5) because the c3-knight would be pinned.

86　Bxh7+ uncovers a winning attack to d4

FRENCH DEFENSE　**1.** e4　e6　**2.** d4　d5　**3.** Nd2　dxe4
　　　　　　　　　4. Nxe4　Be7　**5.** Nf3　Nf6
　　　　　　　　　6. Nxf6+　Bxf6　**7.** Bd3　0-0
　　　　　　　　　8. 0-0　Bxd4

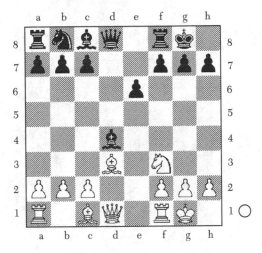

WHITE TO MOVE

Winning way: White annexes a piece with **9. Nxd4.** If Black should be so bold as to take back on d4 with his queen, the sacrifice of White's bishop on h7—with check!—unveils a winning discovery to Black's queen.

How, what, and why: Black could try to steal a pawn by 7. . . . Bxd4, but that fails to 8. Nxd4 Qxd4 9. Bb5+, discovering triumphantly on d4. So to avoid this misstep, Black instead castles, thinking it gets his king to safety and avoids this particular discovery. And it does both these things, though it doesn't take into account a different but comparable discovery going in the other direction, toward White's right. Since taking on d4 still loses a piece, a wiser idea on move eight is simply to develop the queen-knight to d7. The moral? Just because the king is castled doesn't mean your position is safe.

87   Bb5+ opens the d-file with tempo

FRENCH DEFENSE   **1.** e4 e6 **2.** d4 d5 **3.** Nc3 Bb4
4. Bd2 dxe4 **5.** Nxe4 Qxd4
6. Bd3 Bxd2+ **7.** Qxd2 Qxb2
8. Rd1 a6

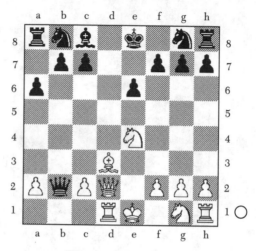

WHITE TO MOVE

Winning way: White assumes command with **9. Bb5+!**. This bolt from the blue uncovers deadly threats along the d-file, such as mate at d8. The best bet for Black is to block at d7, dumping a piece, with White still trashing away.

How, what, and why: White's early pawn sacrifices are speculative, and Black can accept them. But he falters, especially on move eight, unnecessarily guarding b5 against checks. White's doubled power on the d-file enables the bishop to check on this square anyway. If the bishop is taken, White's queen mates at d8, as it does if Black instead blocks the check with a pawn or knight on c6, or even if Black moves the king out of check to e7. Black can survive, however, by interposing on d7. Although White gains a piece (Bb5xd7+) and retains attacking chances, at least Black stays animate.

88   Bxf2+ sets up two different knight forks

CENTER GAME   **1.** e4   e5   **2.** d4   exd4   **3.** Qxd4   Nc6
              4. Qe3   Nf6   **5.** Bc4   Ne5   **6.** Bb3   Bb4+
              7. c3   Bc5   **8.** Qg3

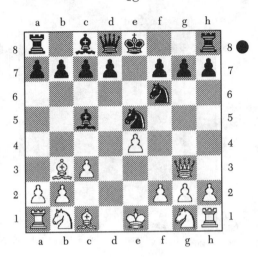

BLACK TO MOVE

Winning way: White's queen is triply forked, starting with **8. . . . Bxf2+!.** If the queen takes the bishop, the e5-knight forks king and queen from d3. And if the king takes the bishop, the f6-knight performs a similar trick on e4.

How, what, and why: Black's first warning shot comes on move seven, when he plays his bishop to c5. If the queen takes the bishop (Qe3xc5), then Black has a knight fork on d3, winning the queen. This arises from White's c-pawn, which was moved to c3 to block the bishop's check on the sixth move. If the pawn were still back on c2, d3 would be guarded, and the e5-knight couldn't enter White's camp. Even with the pawn on c3, White could still defend adequately by retreating the queen to e2 (8. Qe3-e2) instead of g3. With the queen on e2, White could answer Black's bishop sacrifice on f2 by taking with the king, and there'd be no follow-up fork.

89 Bxf2+ sets up Ng4+ and invading at e3

CATALAN OPENING **1.** d4 Nf6 **2.** c4 e6 **3.** Nf3 d5
4. g3 dxc4 **5.** Nbd2 c5 **6.** dxc5 Bxc5
7. Bg2 Bxf2+ **8.** Kxf2 Ng4+ **9.** Ke1

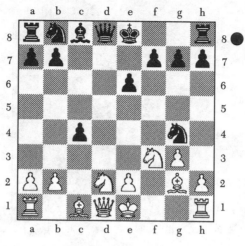

BLACK TO MOVE

Winning way: The fun begins with **9. . . . Ne3.** After White
checks on a4, Black blocks the check with his bishop, forcing the
queen back to a3. A three-way fork to the king, queen, and rook
follows at c2, and White's queen perishes.

How, what, and why: After Black's knight invades on move
eight, White loses no matter where his king retreats. If it goes to
f1, there's a knight fork at e3. If it goes to g1, then Black's queen
checks at d4 and mates in two moves at f2. The problems for
White stem from moves five and six. On the fifth move, White
develops his queen-knight to d2, self-blocking the c1-bishop.
And the exchange on move six (d4xc5) promotes Black's development (6. . . . Bf8xc5). What should White do instead? The oracle
says complete the fianchetto on move five (Bf1-g2) and castle on
move six. At that point, White would be prepared to catch
anything Black can throw.

PHILIDOR DEFENSE   **1.** e4   e5   **2.** Nf3   d6   **3.** d4   Nd7
                   4. Bc4   exd4   **5.** Nxd4   Be7
                   6. Bxf7+!   Kxf7   **7.** Ne6   Kxe6

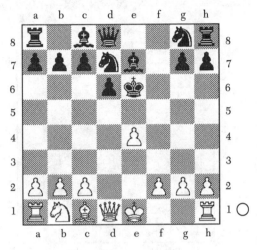

WHITE TO MOVE

Winning way: Black is compelled to take the knight, but White's compulsion is far greater. He gets the king in two moves, starting with **8. Qd5+.** Black's king must decamp to f6, whereupon White's queen finds irresistible mate at f5.

How, what, and why: The key move is the bishop shot 6. Bc4xf7+!. Naturally Black takes it and White invades, 7. Nd4-e6. It turns out better for Black if he doesn't take this knight, but White still gets the upper hand after 7. . . . Qe8 8. Nxc7 Qd8 (if Black answers 8. . . . Qf8, then 9. Qh5+ g6 10. Qd5+ Kf6 11. Bg5+ Kg7 12. Ne6+ wins) 9. Qd5+ Kf8 10. Ne6+, which forks king and queen. Since it's White's light-square control that determines Black's fate, Black might do better on the fourth move by playing either c7-c6 or Ng8-f6, both of which fight for d5 and prevent White's queen from using that square.

KING'S GAMBIT DECLINED **1.** e4 e5 **2.** f4 d6 **3.** Nf3 Nd7
4. Bc4 h6 **5.** 0-0 Be7
6. fxe5 dxe5 **7.** Bxf7+ Kxf7
8. Nxe5+ Ke6 **9.** Qg4+ Kxe5

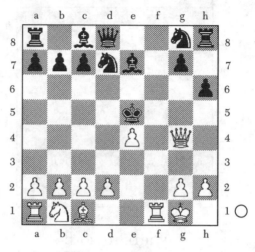

WHITE TO MOVE

Winning way: Mate is fashioned by **10. Qf5+.** Whether the king runs to d6 or to d4, White finishes up with a mating check at d5, smack-dab in the middle of the board.

How, what, and why: This example shows how in the King's Gambit the a2-g8 diagonal and the f-file link up tactically at f7. Black's difficulties are spawned on his fourth move when, to stop White's knight from going to g5, he unnecessarily plays h7-h6. More prudent would be to develop the king-bishop to e7 and then the king-knight to f6. If Black follows these moves by castling, he'll get through the woods. But Little Red Riding Hood plays too cautiously, never activates the king-knight, and partway through the game's journey, Black finds himself lost, like Dante, in a forest of discovered check.

SICILIAN DEFENSE   **1.** e4   c5   **2.** f4   Nc6   **3.** Nf3   g6
                   4. Nc3   Bg7   **5.** Bc4   d6   **6.** 0-0   Bg4

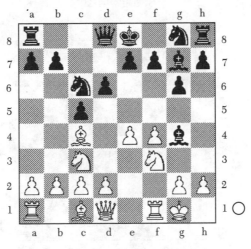

WHITE TO MOVE

Winning way: The g4-bishop is loose change after **7. Bxf7+!.**
Black temporarily gains a piece by taking on f7, but it's a worth-
less gain after the knight checks at g5. Black skips off with his
king, and White's queen pounces on the g4-bishop. The extra
pawn is found money.

How, what, and why: A warning signal should go on when
Black's light-square bishop pins the f3-knight so early, especially
if White has a bishop at c4. It's often possible to sacrifice on f7,
drawing out the king so that it can be checked by a knight
jumping to g5. This breaks the g4-bishop's pin on the f3-knight
with a gain of time, allowing White to expose his queen with
impunity. Black can't take the queen because he must first get
out of check. After the defender moves his king to safety, the
queen takes the bishop.

QUEEN PAWN OPENING   **1.** d4   d5   **2.** Nf3   Nf6   **3.** g3   e6
                 4. Bg5   c5   **5.** dxc5   Bxc5
                 6. Bg2   Bxf2+   **7.** Kxf2

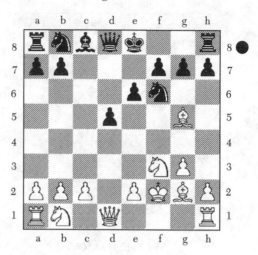

BLACK TO MOVE

Winning way: Black has sacrificed on f2 to draw out White's king. With **7. . . . Ne4+,** Black regains the piece. The king must move to safety, and with the support of its queen, the knight can take the bishop on g5. White loses a pawn and the right to castle.

How, what, and why: White begins to go astray when he trades pawns on move five, d4xc5, which helps build Black's game (Bf8xc5). Better is to continue his own development, flanking his bishop at g2 to expedite castling. In the opening, aim to increase your development while deterring your opponent's. One tactical point: In similar situations where the bishop is sacrificed on f2, Black must decide on which square to check with the f6-knight, g4 or e4. Here, because the g5-bishop is protected by the f3-knight, Black needs to check on e4 so that his queen and knight ally their power against g5.

94   Nxe5 sets up Legal's Mate with two knights and bishop

PHILIDOR DEFENSE   **1.** e4 e5 **2.** Nf3 d6 **3.** Bc4 Bg4
    4. Nc3 h6

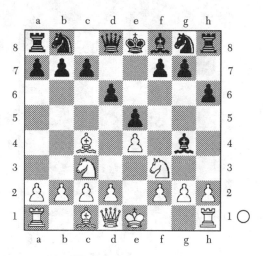

WHITE TO MOVE

Winning way: White surrenders his queen with **5. Nxe5!.** Black says, "What's this?" He takes White's queen and White follows with a bishop check on f7. The king moves up to e7 and White's queen-knight mates at d5—a ménage of three minor pieces known as Legal's Mate.

How, what, and why: This attack is named after Legall de Kermeur (1702–92), usually shortened to Legal, Philidor's chess teacher. Black thinks he has a solid pin on White's f3-knight, but the pin is illusory, which is bared by White's fifth move (Nf3xe5). However, instead of taking the queen and allowing Legal's Mate, Black should settle for losing a pawn by taking on e5. He falters particularly with two moves: the third (Bc8-g4), a premature pin, and the fourth (h7-h6), a weakening and useless pawn move. Black is better served by developing the kingside minor pieces and castling. At least these avoid losing in seven moves.

95   Nxe4 sets up Legal's Mate with two bishops and knight

PETROFF DEFENSE   **1.** e4 e5   **2.** Nf3 Nf6   **3.** Nxe5 Nc6
4. Nxc6 dxc6   **5.** d3 Bc5   **6.** Bg5

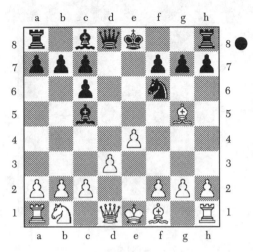

BLACK TO MOVE

Winning way: Black breaks the pin and White's back with **6. . . . Nxe4!.** If White takes the queen (7. Bg5xd8), Black's king-bishop checks on f2, driving the enemy king to e2, whereupon the queen-bishop mates on g4—a version of Legal's Mate involving two bishops and a knight.

How, what, and why: On move seven, instead of downing Black's queen (Bg5xd8), White could take Black's knight (d3xe4). This also fails, however, for Black has a deflective bishop sacrifice on f2. White loses his queen whether he captures the bishop or not. If he takes the bishop (Ke1xf2), Black's queen just takes White's (Qd8xd1). And if White moves his king to e2, his two most important pieces are skewered by a bishop check on g4. Once again, the prematurely developed queen-bishop (6. Bc1-g5) is the source of the trouble.

96   Nxe4 sets up Legal's Mate with bishop and knight

ALAPIN'S OPENING   **1.** e4   e5   **2.** Ne2   Bc5   **3.** d3   Nf6
                            4. Bg5

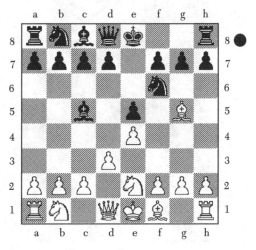

BLACK TO MOVE

Winning way: It's a pin, but White shouldn't pin his hopes on it after **4. . . . Nxe4!.** Take Black's queen, and Black mates at f2. White's best move is to admit the error and retreat, 5. Bg5-e3, leaving him down by a pawn but still able to pin again.

How, what, and why: White's poor judgment (pinning prematurely) is exacerbated by the feeble development of the king-knight to e2. From there, the knight clogs White's position and fails to perform its knightly duty of guarding the g5-bishop, which it does admirably from f3. Instead of the half-baked bishop development to g5, White has several ways to proceed on move four, including shifting his e2-knight to g3 and then lifting his king-bishop to e2, after which castling kingside glows promisingly. But the actual joust (4. Bc1-g5) leads to the dark ages.

Nxe5 discovers on h5 and sets up Legal's Mate

RUY LOPEZ   **1.** e4   e5   **2.** Nf3   Nc6   **3.** Bb5   a6
4. Ba4   Nge7   **5.** Nc3   d6   **6.** Nd5   b5
7. Bb3   Bg4   **8.** h3   Bh5

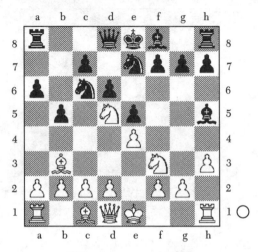

WHITE TO MOVE

Winning way: Black is stupefied by **9. Nxe5!**. If he takes either knight, White's queen eliminates the hapless bishop on h5. And if he predaciously grabs White's queen (9. . . . Bh5xd1), mate ensues: 10. Nf6+ gxf6 11. Bxf7#.

How, what, and why: This is a more complex case of Legal's artifice. The first crossroads comes on move eight, when White drives the bishop to h5. This is necessary, for if White sacrifices (Nf3xe5) with the bishop still on g4, Black's c6-knight can recapture on e5, upholding the bishop against White's queen. The next critical juncture is move ten. Since the b3-bishop is obstructed by White's own d5-knight, the steed must be jettisoned. The throwaway 10. Nd5-f6+ serves admirably. It clears the b3-f7 diagonal with tempo (with check). Supported by the e5-knight, the unveiled bishop mates by capturing on f7.

♔

Knight Discoveries and Exploiting the e-file

In Chapter Eight, seventeen examples present a variety of stratagems, falling into two groups: knight moves other than Legal's Mate that result in discovered attacks, and a number of devices that capitalize on a vulnerable e-file. Rooks join the fight in this latter grouping in several instances, and most of the examples concern the gain of material. Checkmates are less common, though there are just enough thrown in to whet the appetite. Pins, skewers, forks, discoveries and double checks, undermining—all the major tactics of chess are depicted. Check it out.

PETROFF DEFENSE   **1.** e4   e5   **2.** Nf3   Nf6   **3.** d3   d6
                     4. Nbd2   Nc6   **5.** Be2   Bg4   **6.** 0-0   Nd4

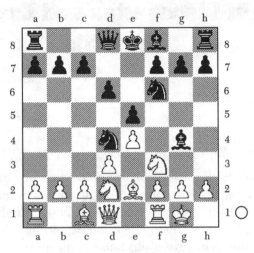

WHITE TO MOVE

Winning way: Black is battered by **7. Nxd4,** when taking the knight (7. . . . e5xd4) enables the g4-bishop to be captured with the queen's support. Meanwhile, trying to save the bishop by trading it (7. . . . Bg4xe2) allows the retrieval of the d4-knight (8. Nd4xe2!), and White stays a piece ahead.

How, what, and why: This example illustrates another way to discover an attack along the d1-h5 diagonal. The queen-bishop on g4 is still one of the targets, but instead of e5 (and eventually f7), the other sitting duck is the square d4 and whatever sits on it (in this case, Black's venturesome knight). The tactic of taking on d4 (Nf3xd4) works because of the discovered double threat to g4 and the fact that the d4-knight can come back to recapture on e2, reclaiming itself before Black can take it.

FRENCH DEFENSE   **1.** e4   e6   **2.** d4   d5   **3.** e5   c5
                 4. c3   Nc6   **5.** Bb5   Bd7   **6.** Nf3

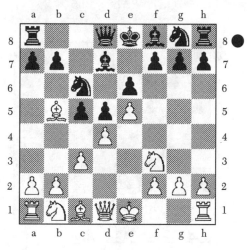

BLACK TO MOVE

Winning way: Black capitalizes on White's undefended b5-bishop with the discovery **6. . . . Nxe5!**. If White takes back on e5, he loses his bishop on b5. And if White swaps bishops (Bb5xd7+), trying to obtain equal value for his bishop before retaking on e5, Black recaptures with his menaced knight (Ne5xd7) before White has a chance to take it. Black gets two for one, emerging a pawn ahead.

How, what, and why: White veers off course with 5. Bf1-b5, because this could lead to an unfavorable trade of light-square bishops: White's good one for Black's bad one. And if White instead trades bishop for knight (Bb5xc6), Black recaptures with the b7-pawn and his bad bishop can deploy at a6, striking deep into White's position. Of course, White's sixth move allows a costly unpinning combination. To avoid this, White could trade bishop for knight (Bb5xc6) or defend b5 (a2-a4, for example).

RUY LOPEZ **1.** e4 e5 **2.** Nf3 Nc6 **3.** Bb5 a6
4. Bxc6 dxc6 **5.** Nc3 f6 **6.** d3 Bg4
7. Be3 Qd7 **8.** h3 Bh5

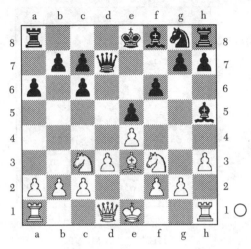

WHITE TO MOVE

Winning way: It's queen for queen after **9. Nxe5!**. After 9. . . . Bxd1 10. Nxd7 Bxc2 11. Nxf8 Kxf8, White corrals a bishop with the kingly 12. Kd2. Meanwhile, if Black averts the queenly trade and takes White's knight, 9. . . . f6xe5, White has the last word chessically with 10. Qxh5+.

How, what, and why: Here's another case of a tactic needing proper preparation. The unpinning combination, where both queens hang, fails if White plays it earlier, on move eight. It doesn't work because Black's queen defends the g4-bishop. If 8. Nxe5, Black can simply take the knight (f6xe5) and that's that. So the bishop must be driven back to an undefended square (h5). Once that's accomplished (8. h2-h3 Bg4-h5), White can discover on the bishop by capturing on e5, and the tactic succeeds. Obviously, to be a tactical wizard, one cannot ignore timing.

Nd5 discovers on a5

CENTER COUNTER DEFENSE **1.** e4 d5 **2.** exd5 Qxd5
3. Nc3 Qa5 **4.** d4 Nf6
5. Bc4 g6 **6.** Bd2 Bg7

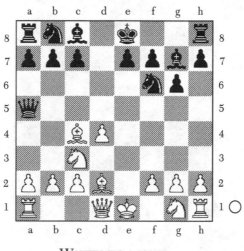

WHITE TO MOVE

Winning way: You can put Black in an imbroglio with **7. Nd5.**
After only one move, he can't both save the queen and stop the
knight fork at c7. Worse, he must lose his queen. If he moves it to
a4, White's bishop checks on b5. The queen takes it, but the
knight administers a royal fork at c7, leaving Black feeling less
than regal.

How, what, and why: A queen on the edge has a big circum-
ference but a short radius. The moment White plays his bishop
to d2, Black should move the c-pawn to c6, giving the queen a
diagonal of retreat. But Black's actual sixth move, Bf8-g7,
blithely ignores the problem, which is Black's poorly placed
queen. This example shows that the same power of diagonal
discovery used to triumph on the kingside (from d1 to h5) can
shine equally on the queenside, along the a5-e1 diagonal.

QUEEN PAWN GAME   **1.** d4   Nf6   **2.** Nf3   e6   **3.** g3   b6
                     4. Bg2   Bb7   **5.** 0-0   Be7   **6.** Bg5   d6
                     7. Qd3   0-0

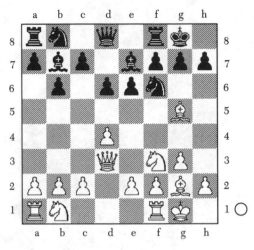

WHITE TO MOVE

Winning way: First a setup move, **8. Bxf6.** After Black takes back, White has 9. Nf3-g5, discovering on b7 and threatening mate at h7. Black thwarts the mate, but White takes on b7 and then a8, acquiring the exchange (rook for minor piece).

How, what, and why: This is a clear case of "castling into it," where Black thinks that he's safeguarding his king by castling, but is actually placing it in greater danger. By taking on f6, White removes Black's sentinel, weakening h7. After Black takes back (8. . . . Be7xf6), White's knight goes to g5 even though that hangs it. Black commandeers it to stop the mate (9. . . . Bf6xg5), but there are consequences. White's unveiled bishop plays the old one-two (Bg2xb7 and Bb7xa8), accruing two pawns' worth of value on the deal. This example is a reminder that castling isn't always propitious. Sometimes it's better to delay castling, to castle the other way, or not to castle at all.

SCOTCH GAME   **1.** e4   e5   **2.** Nf3   Nc6   **3.** d4   exd4
              4. Nxd4   Bc5   **5.** Be3   Nf6

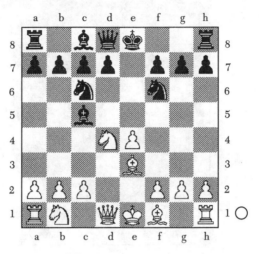

WHITE TO MOVE

Winning way: White has a masked attack on c5. After **6. Nxc6,** Black is unable to take back without losing his c5-bishop. And he can't spend a move to save the bishop (Bc5xe3) because the invading knight attacks his queen. He has little choice but to retake on c6, allowing White to plunder the bishop.

How, what, and why: Return to the scene of the crime—Black's fifth move, Ng8-f6. This ignores White's previous move, Bc1-e3. Sure, it appears that with the development of the queen-bishop, White is merely bolstering his centralized knight. But actually he's drawing the bow on a potential discovery to the c5-bishop. The best answer is for Black's menaced piece to fall back to b6, where it's securely guarded by two pawns. Development is important, but it shouldn't outweigh the requirements of sound play. If threats are real, they must be answered.

SICILIAN DEFENSE   **1.** e4   c5   **2.** Nf3   e6   **3.** d4   cxd4
     4. Nxd4   Nc6   **5.** Nc3   a6   **6.** Be2   Qc7
     7. Be3   Bc5

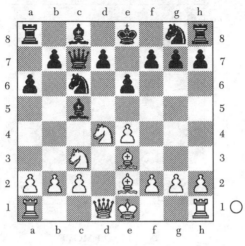

WHITE TO MOVE

Winning way: Any movement of the d4-knight uncovers an attack to c5, but only one earns material: **8. Nxe6!**. Since this bodacious knight attacks both queen and bishop, Black must obliterate it, but this doesn't save the c5-bishop. White devours it and goes up a pawn on the entire transaction.

How, what, and why: Putting the bishop on c5 is a rotten strategy, inasmuch as it may be discovered upon at any point. A safer plan is to develop it to e7, speeding up castling. At least this scheme avoids material loss while enabling Black to deploy his forces adequately. In fact, it's possible to see the discovery and still fall for it, thinking that the threat is to play 8. Nd4xc6. Since Black has the reasonable reply 8. . . . Qc7xc6, guarding the c5-bishop, he might conclude that there's nothing to fear. But the real threat is to take on e6, not c6, and this what Black misses.

105   Nxc6 discovers check on e-file

RUY LOPEZ   **1.** e4   e5   **2.** Nf3   Nc6   **3.** Bb5   Nf6
           4. 0-0   Nxe4   **5.** Re1   Nd6   **6.** Nc3   Nxb5
           7. Nxe5   Nxc3

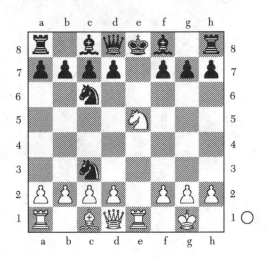

WHITE TO MOVE

Winning way: White has set the bait and starts to reel in the fish with **8. Nxc6+.** Black answers the discovered check by blocking with the bishop at e7. After 9. Nxe7! Nxd1 10. Ng6+, Black is forced to interpose his queen. The final finesse is 11. Nxe7!. This knight escapes, and the Black one at d1 doesn't.

How, what, and why: The warning sign is White's rook on e1. It's poised on the same file as Black's king, with no pawn sheltering His Majesty from a discovery. In order to survive, Black must relocate quickly to get his king to safety. The last chance occurs at move six. Here, Black should develop the king-bishop to e7 and then castle. But instead he takes White's b5-bishop, and the rest is chess-tory.

KING'S GAMBIT ACCEPTED **1.** e4 e5 **2.** f4 exf4 **3.** Nf3 d5
4. Nc3 dxe4 **5.** Nxe4 Bg4
6. Qe2 Bxf3

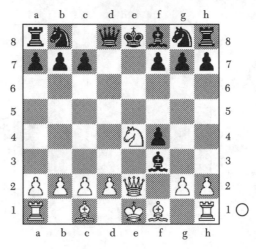

WHITE TO MOVE

Winning way: White's queen may be assailed, but there's no denying that **7. Nf6#!** is check. In fact, it's double check and mate.

How, what, and why: Trouble for Black doesn't start rearing its head until the premature development of the queen-bishop on move five. Since the center is open, Black should be endeavoring to castle kingside expeditiously, which means the kingside pieces should be mobilized first. The nail in the coffin, however, is Black's next move, 6. . . . Bg4xf3?. Superficially this looks okay because of the attack to White's queen, but the ensuing double check (7. Ne4-f6#) vitiates the defender's best-laid plans. Although both checking units (the queen and knight) are themselves attacked, neither can be taken by virtue of the double check. Since the knight also guards the potential escape square at d7, that's all, folks.

107 Bb4# discovers mate by double check

FRENCH DEFENSE   **1.** e4   e6   **2.** d4   d5   **3.** Nc3   dxe4
                        4. Nxe4   Nd7   **5.** Nf3   Ngf6
                        6. Nfg5   Be7   **7.** Nxf7   Kxf7
                        8. Ng5+   Kg8   **9.** Nxe6   Qe8   **10.** Nxc7

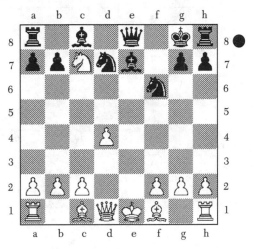

BLACK TO MOVE

Winning way: Black's queen and rook are forked, but this means nothing after **10. . . . Bb4#!**. Black moves only one piece, but it's a two-timing double check and discovered mate.

How, what, and why: White plays this attack with blinders on. When Black seemingly ignores the upstart invasion 6. Nf3-g5 by developing his king-bishop (instead of driving away the knight with h7-h6), White should pause to ponder the consequences of his contemplated sacrifice on f7 more rigorously. Never assume that your opponent has merely fallen into your envisioned trap without giving your analysis the once-over. To this end, after careful scrutiny of the intended variation, do one last thing before playing it. Ask yourself: "Are there any checks that could upset my plans?" Do this as a matter of course, and you will be surprised how often it saves you from looking foolish.

108   Nxc3+ discovers check on the e-file

VIENNA GAME   **1.** e4   e5   **2.** Nc3   Bc5   **3.** Nf3   d6
4. d4   exd4   **5.** Nxd4   Nf6   **6.** Bc4   0-0
7. Bg5   Re8   **8.** f3   Nxe4   **9.** Bxd8

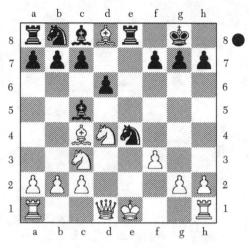

BLACK TO MOVE

Winning way: Black's queen-behind situation is ephemeral after **9. . . . Nxc3+!**. Moreover, the raven emerges a piece ahead, and White has no surcease of sorrow.

How, what, and why: White fumbles on move eight. Since Black has just played his rook to the e-file (7. . . . Rf8-e8), a latent discovery is in the chilled air. White should see the signs and, instead of depending on the shaky protection 8. f2-f3, castle. The next warning signal is set off at move nine, after White has already dropped a pawn. Here he should minimize his loss by 9. Nc3xe4, though Black stays on top with 9. . . . Qxg5. But White materialistically takes the queen, 10. Bg5xd8, overlooking Black's in-between tactic, 10. . . . Ne4xc3+, a discovered check on the e-file. Since the check must be answered, White's queen is lost, and Black comes out a piece ahead.

Bxe4 sets up Rel pin

RUY LOPEZ **1.** e4 e5 **2.** Nf3 Nc6 **3.** Bb5 Nf6
  4. 0-0 Nxe4 **5.** d4 a6 **6.** Bd3 d5
  7. c4 exd4 **8.** cxd5 Qxd5

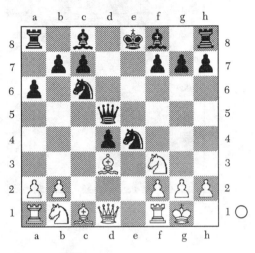

WHITE TO MOVE

Winning way: Black can declare bankruptcy after **9. Bxe4.** He can then stagger away with his queen, remaining a piece to the bad, or take back on e4, which loses the queen to the battering pin of the rook once it moves to e1. It's a hard-knock life.

How, what, and why: Maybe he won't go from rags to riches, but on move seven Black can avoid debtor's prison by taking on d4, though with a different unit. Instead of capturing with the pawn, 7. . . . e5xd4, which renders two knights precarious after 8. c4xd5, Black should counter with 7. . . . Nc6xd4!. In this case, 8. Nf3xd4 e5xd4 9. c4xd5 leaves only one knight in danger, the one on e4, and it can retreat to f6. Then, if White checks along the e-file, Black can develop his king-bishop to e7 with the aim of castling. No Bill Gates fortune here, but it avoids the soup lines.

RUY LOPEZ   **1.** e4   e5   **2.** Nf3   Nc6   **3.** Bb5   Nf6   **4.** d3   a6

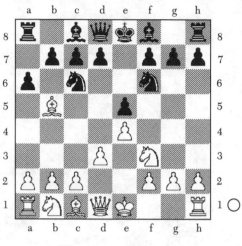

WHITE TO MOVE

Winning way: White wins a pawn by **5. Bxc6.** No matter how Black takes back, White's f3-knight captures the e5-pawn, laughing all the way to the blankety-blank.

How, what, and why: Black's advance a7-a6 is ill-timed. It should come before White has had an extra move to protect his e-pawn, on move three, not move four. If, after 3. . . . a7-a6, White exchanges bishop for knight (4. Bb5xc6 d7xc6) in an attempt to win the king-pawn (5. Nf3xe5), Black can regain the pawn by doubly attacking e4 and e5 with 5. . . . Qd8-d4. But if the rook-pawn's advance is delayed till move four, the counter Qd8-d4 fails. Since in the interim White has had time to guard e4 with a pawn (d2-d3), the invading queen issues only a single attack, to e5. White retreats his knight to f3, out of danger and ahead by a pawn.

RUY LOPEZ   **1.** e4   e5   **2.** Nf3   Nc6   **3.** Bb5   a6
             4. Ba4   Nf6   **5.** 0-0   d6   **6.** Re1   b5
             7. Bb3   Na5   **8.** d4   exd4   **9.** e5   dxe5
             10. Nxe5   Be6

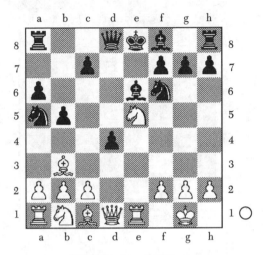

WHITE TO MOVE

Winning way: The *übermensch* becomes the under-*mensch* with **11. Nxf7!**, undermining the support for e6. Black loses a pawn, the right to castle, and any hope for the good life.

How, what, and why: Black's problems begin on move seven, with the knight's sortie to the edge of the board, Nc6-a5. Although this attack aims at the b3-bishop, it abandons the center to the forces that be, and they dragoon their way with the thrusts d2-d4 and e4-e5. Still, Black could bail out by completing what he starts. That is, he could remove the belligerent bishop at b3 on move eight. Failing that, his equivocation leads him to play 10. . . . Bc8-e6, upholding f7 and obstructing the e-file from White's militant rook. But the stopgap is only temporary, and Black's makeshift barricade topples on a knight sacrifice.

FOUR KNIGHTS GAME   **1.** e4 e5 **2.** Nf3 Nc6 **3.** Nc3 Nf6
                    4. Bb5 Bb4 **5.** a3 Be7 **6.** 0-0 0-0
                    7. Bxc6 dxc6 **8.** Nxe5 Nxe4
                    9. Nxe4 Qd4

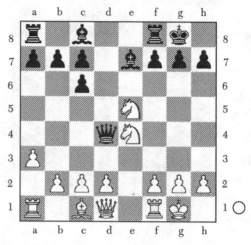

WHITE TO MOVE

Winning way: White can save the right knight with **10. Nf3!** (moving the other one fails to win the e7-bishop). That leaves the e4-knight in place, and if Black takes it, his queen and bishop are skewered by 11. Re1. The queen will then move to safety and the bishop is extinguished, 12. Re1xe7.

How, what, and why: Black's indirect defense of the e5-pawn starts to come apart when he castles, which leaves the e7-bishop with only one defender, the queen. But the queen's services are required elsewhere, at d4 to give a double attack, and this leaves the bishop without visible means of support and prone to e-file tactics. Strangely, Black might "save" the bishop (at least its value) by trading it for a knight on move five (Bb4xc3). After all, how can you lose what doesn't exist?

QUEEN'S GAMBIT DECLINED   **1.** d4   d5   **2.** c4   e6
                             3. Nc3   c5   **4.** cxd5   exd5
                             5. dxc5   d4   **6.** Ne4   f5
                             7. Ng3   Qa5+   **8.** Bd2   Qxc5

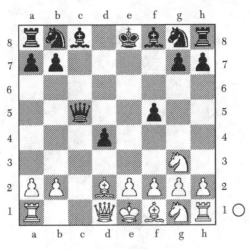

WHITE TO MOVE

Winning way: Black is in trouble after **9. Rc1.** The queen is attacked, and so is the bishop behind it. That's a skewer, and the queen can't save itself and rescue the bishop with the same move.

How, what, and why: On move seven, there's no need to check with the queen to regain the c-pawn. Black's f8-bishop can recapture it immediately, 7. . . . Bf8xc5. But once Black's queen does check (7. . . . Qd8-a5+), and White blocks the check with the bishop (8. Bc1-d2), Her Majesty is compelled to move again. At this point, Black should admit the error and retreat the queen to safety. This cedes the c5-pawn to White, but at least it averts a humbling c-file skewer. This is a problem that tends to plague most students: overkill, using the queen to achieve what can be realized by less force.

Sicilian Defense   **1.** e4   c5   **2.** d4   cxd4   **3.** c3   dxc3
            4. Nxc3   Nc6   **5.** Bc4   d6   **6.** Nf3   Nf6
            7. e5   dxe5   **8.** Qxd8+   Nxd8
            9. Nb5   Kd7

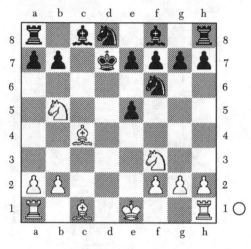

WHITE TO MOVE

Winning way: Two knight checks do the trick. The first one, **10. Nxe5+,** drives Black's king back to its cubbyhole, e8. The second check, 11. Nc7#, has a tragic, final quality about it, as does any checkmate.

How, what, and why: Curiously, after trading queens White's attack does not ebb. Once Black's queen is gone, White's queen-knight gains mastery over c7. Another paradox occurs when Black preserves the right to castle by taking back on d8 with his c6-knight. This turns out to be a negative, for with the knight so obstructive, Black's king winds up defending by using d7 instead of d8. The result is that White's knights check it back to the Stone Age. Just because a principle usually holds doesn't mean it always does. Sometimes it's prudent to forfeit the right to castle.

♚

Smothering Knights and Cross-Firing Bishops

Another big section, Chapter Nine offers nineteen illustrations of bishop-and-knight play at its best. There are attacks to c7 (c2 for Black), pins along the a4-e8 diagonal (the a5-e1 diagonal for Black), smothering knight invasions at d6 and e6 (d3 and e3 for Black knights), tricky raids with knights and bishops moving to g5 (g4 for Black), and several bust-up shots around the castled king's position. Pile on a few diagonal checkmates and have some fun.

Bf5 with Nd4 wins on c2

TERRORIST ATTACK   **1.** e4 e5 **2.** Qh5 Nc6 **3.** Bc4 g6
                         4. Qf3 Nf6 **5.** g3 Nd4 **6.** Qd3 d5
                         7. exd5

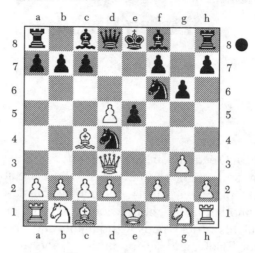

BLACK TO MOVE

Winning way: White's queen is distressed after **7. . . . Bf5.** If it draws back to f1, White is embarrassed by a knight fork at c2. If 8. Qc3, then 8. . . . Bb4 9. Qxb4 Nxc2+ is even more incommodious, to say nothing of 9. Qe3 Nxc2+.

How, what, and why: White tries for a quick knockout, aiming for a Scholar's Mate at f7. But Black's pieces rebuff this unsound assault, and White's queen is driven back, eventually constrained to uphold c2 from d3. With the d-pawn so blocked, White's queenside development is hindered, and the limited maneuverability reduces the clumsy queen to Quasimodo status. As bad as this is, White should not take Black's d-pawn. Better to withdraw the bishop to b3, securing c2. But White takes the pawn (7. e4xd5) and is squelched by 7. . . . Bc8-f5. After 8. Qd2-c3 Bf8-b4, Black's knight has a royal fork at c2, and the queen is no longer Esmeralda.

EVANS GAMBIT ACCEPTED   **1.** e4 e5 **2.** Nf3 Nc6
                        3. Bc4 Bc5 **4.** b4 Nxb4
                        5. Nxe5 Qf6 **6.** d4

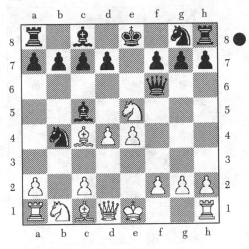

BLACK TO MOVE

Winning way: The stitches unravel with **6. . . . Bxd4!.** If White takes the bishop, **8. Qd1xd4,** the queen is lost by a knight-fork at c2. Meanwhile, how does White answer the threats to a1, e5, and f2? He doesn't.

How, what, and why: White's miscalculation is based on an overload error, where the queen cannot guard both d4 and c2 simultaneously. If called upon to defend d4, it will be out of position to guard c2 and vulnerable itself. But it's the knight capture at e5 that precipitates the crisis. White should instead drive back Black's intrusive knight by 5. c2-c3. (As a rule, never let an enemy piece idle in your half of the board.) Then White should continue with 6. d2-d4, blunting the c5-bishop and establishing a center typical of the Evans Gambit.

117 Bb4 pins the queen and deflects it from c2

BISHOP'S OPENING   **1.** e4   e5   **2.** Bc4   Nc6   **3.** Qf3   Qf6
                 4. Qc3   Nd4   **5.** d3

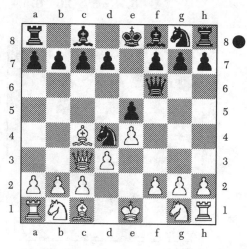

BLACK TO MOVE

Winning way: White's queen and king are on the same diagonal, which is perfect for the pinning **5. . . . Bb4!**. The only way to try to save the queen is to take the bishop, but that falters to a follow-up knight fork at c2.

How, what, and why: White's halfhearted attempt at a four-move checkmate is countered by Black's offer to trade queens. Inexperienced players don't like conducting a chess game without a queen, thinking they need it to implement their plans. But how can one expect to handle the queen artfully without first appreciating its component parts? Here White refuses Black's proposed exchange (3. . . . Qd8-f6), transferring the queen to c3 just to keep it on the board. Unfortunately, a move later it disappears anyway—lost for a bishop! In your own play, try to get practice using the little pieces. You may need to call upon them someday, and it helps to know what they do.

118 Nc2+ forces mate with four minor pieces

QUEEN'S GAMBIT DECLINED   **1.** d4   d5   **2.** Nf3   Bf5
                          3. c4   e6   **4.** Nc3   Nf6
                          5. Qb3 Nc6 **6.** Qxb7 Nb4
                          7. Nb5 Ne4 **8.** Nxc7+ Qxc7
                          9. Qxc7

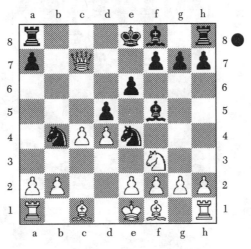

BLACK TO MOVE

Winning way: Black wins with **9. . . . Nc2+.** This forces 10. Kd1 Nxf2+ 11. Kd2 Bb4#—mate with four minor pieces, and White doesn't get last licks.

How, what, and why: White tries to take advantage of Black's early development of the queen-bishop, aiming at the undefended b7-pawn (5. Qd1-b3). But the queen-knight pawn, typically identified as the "poisoned pawn," can lead to a bellyache if swallowed, especially in Her Majesty's tummy. Here the enemy minor pieces frolic on c2, the square abandoned by White's queen. The big surprise is Black's queen sacrifice on move eight. Who needs a queen with a troupe of congenial minor pieces working in perfect harmony?

SICILIAN DEFENSE   **1.** e4   c5   **2.** Nf3   Nc6   **3.** d4   cxd4
                    4. Nxd4   e6   **5.** Nc3   a6   **6.** Be3   Qc7
                    7. Qd2   Bd6

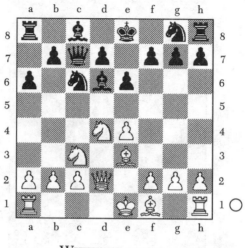

WHITE TO MOVE

Winning way: White has a grand old time with **8. Ndb5!**, forking queen and bishop. Black gets one knight, 8. . . . a6xb5, but its replacement arrives, 9. Nc3xb5, and after Black saves his queen, 9. Nb5xd6+ regains the piece, putting White a pawn ahead with a strong attack.

How, what, and why: For the opening setup Black has in mind, the advance a7-a6 is a necessary adjunct, providing security for Black's queen when it comes to c7, which it often does in the Sicilian. On move seven, Black is okay after Ng8-f6. But the erroneous 7. . . . Bf8-d6 strains the position to the breaking point. In fact, White wins by invading with either knight to b5. For example, if instead 8. Nc3-b5, and Black tries to survive with 8. . . . Qc7-b8, White has the brusque 9. Nd4xc6 and 10. Nb5xd6+—ouch.

SICILIAN DEFENSE   **1.** e4   c5   **2.** d4   cxd4   **3.** c3   dxc3
               4. Nxc3   e6   **5.** Nf3   Qc7
               6. Nb5   Qa5+   **7.** Bd2   Bb4

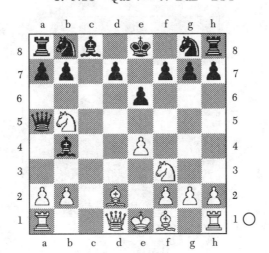

WHITE TO MOVE

Winning way: Black's b4-bishop is pinned along the a5-d2 diagonal, which means White can play **8. Nd6+** in a risk-free environment. Whether Black moves his king to e7 or f8, White's knight takes on c8. Thanks much. And if the king sidles instead to d8, then the knight has a fork at f7. Much thanks.

How, what, and why: It seems that Black's bishop on b4 holds d6. But it's pinned, shielding its own queen from White's d2-bishop. Thus, it's Black who signals his own demise by interposing the dark-square bishop into a pin on move seven. His cause could be helped if he simply retreats his queen to d8. This avoids the pin and enables the f8-bishop to retain power over d6. If White then invades with the knight, the unpinned bishop can take it. That's all it takes—staying out of the pin.

121   Bxc2 sets up Nd3# smothered mate

QUEEN PAWN OPENING   **1.** d4   d5   **2.** e3   Bf5   **3.** Ne2   e6
                      4. Nbc3   Nc6   **5.** Rc1   Nb4   **6.** Bd2

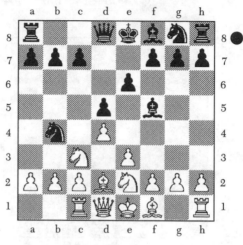

BLACK TO MOVE

Winning way: Chess and life become unbearable for White after **6. . . . Bxc2!**. Either White surrenders his queen or tries to save it, 7. Rc1xc2, allowing 7. . . . Nb4-d3#—a smotherino.

How, what, and why: White's opening scheme, if we can call it that, involves a whole string of second-rate moves, adding up to one very bad plan. The final straw is 6. Bc1-d2. This dullish development must lead to material loss. Change White's sixth move to Ne2-g3, obtaining some breathing space, and White's position becomes playable. His f1-bishop can then come out and his king gets a little air. In the end, however, White is suffocated by central congestion.

122 Ne3 wins queen or deflects f2 for mate

QUEEN PAWN GAME   **1.** d4   Nf6   **2.** Nd2   e5   **3.** dxe5   Ng4
           4. h3

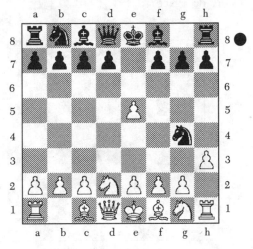

BLACK TO MOVE

Winning way: Black's knight can move forward winningly with
4. . . . Ne3!. If the knight is taken, Black has a Fool's Mate along
the e1-h4 diagonal. Otherwise, White's queen departs.

How, what, and why: Things start down a wayward path with
White's second move, after which his queen-knight obstructs the
c1-bishop's control of e3. But the actual losing move is White's
fourth play, h2-h3. This push attacks the knight at the expense of
the square g3, which can never again (this game) be guarded by
the h-pawn. A superior try would be the developing move 4.
Ng1-f3, defending the e-pawn and adding protection to h4,
making certain that the Black queen isn't able to invade on this
square. Black's winning sacrifice (4. . . . Ng4-e3) is a deflection to
lure the f2-pawn out of position, hoping to open the e1-h4
diagonal. After Black's fourth move, White has no hope and
should resign.

123   Ne6 wins the queen because of pin

RUY LOPEZ   **1.** e4   e5   **2.** Nf3   Nc6   **3.** Bb5   Bc5
                4. c3   f5   **5.** d4   fxe4   **6.** Ng5   Bb6
                7. d5   Nce7

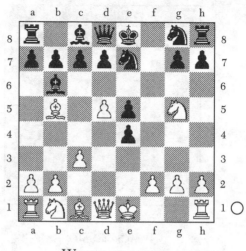

WHITE TO MOVE

Winning way: Black is a little too cozy. White snuggles in with **8. Ne6!**. This smothers the queen, for the d7-pawn is pinned under the blanket by the not so slumbrous b5-bishop.

How, what, and why: Sharp play is initiated by Black's fourth move, f7-f5, after which the slightest slip can be instantly fatal for either side. When White attacks the c6-knight by advancing the d-pawn, 7. d4-d5, Black's knight should retreat to b8 and redeploy. But withdrawing to the back rank tends to negate previous development, so Black naturally transfers his knight to e7 instead, hoping to shift to g6 or f5. But this normal-looking maneuver congests Black's middle, and with the d7-pawn being inoperative because of the b5-bishop's pin, e6 is not guarded and therefore available to White's handy g5-knight. It enters and triumphs over the queen (Ng5-e6 and Ne6xd8).

QUEEN PAWN GAME   **1.** d4   d5   **2.** Nf3   Bg4   **3.** Nbd2   e6
                     4. Ne5   Bf5   **5.** c3   c5   **6.** Qa4+   Nd7

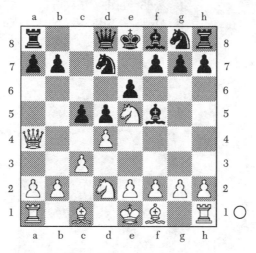

WHITE TO MOVE

Winning way: White sagely defers exchanging on d7 until **7. e4!.** Regardless how Black saves the bishop, White takes on d7 with his knight. If Black's queen takes back, it gets pinned by the light-square bishop. White wins a piece.

How, what, and why: Black's c-pawn push is premature. After the pawn moves to c5, it no longer can block the a4-e8 diagonal by going to c6. To exploit this loosening, White needs to introduce the light-square bishop, which means the e-pawn must be moved. Advance it one square, however, and Black has time to guard b5 with his rook-pawn, a7-a6. White gains a tempo, though, by advancing his e-pawn two squares, snarling at Black's light-square bishop. This loses the e-pawn (d5xe4 or Bf5xe4), but the sacrifice is inconsequential. More important is the time gained by forcing Black to take the pawn, to save the f5-bishop. Black is unable to play a7-a6, and White pilfers a piece.

QUEEN PAWN GAME

	1.	d4	d5	2.	Nf3	c6	3.	c4	Nf6
	4.	Nc3	Bf5	5.	Bg5	Ne4			
	6.	cxd5	cxd5	7.	Qb3	Qa5			
	8.	Qxd5	Qxd5	9.	Nxd5	Na6			
	10.	e3	e6						

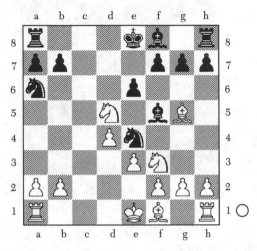

WHITE TO MOVE

Winning way: White's knight is attacked and it can't penetrate behind the lines at c7, which is guarded by the knight at a6. But here the race is to the bishops. With **11. Bb5#**, a mate is produced by the crossing action of two bishops.

How, what, and why: Black's problems originate with the early development of the queen-bishop. He can counter by inserting a knight-exchange on move six (6. . . . Ne4xc3) before retaking on d5. Even as late as move ten, Black could stay afloat by moving his rook to c8. But 10. . . . e7-e6, while it attacks the d5-knight, lamentably opens the d8-g5 diagonal, activating the dark-square bishop. The light-square bishop then provides the high point, 11. Bf1-b5#!.

QUEEN'S GAMBIT DECLINED   **1.** d4   d5   **2.** c4   e6
                        3. Nc3   Nf6   **4.** Bg5   Nbd7
                        5. cxd5   exd5   **6.** Nxd5

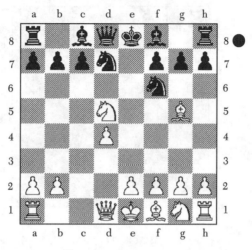

BLACK TO MOVE

Winning way: White tries to snake off with the d5-pawn, but the pin can be shed by **6. . . . Nxd5!**, allowing 7. Bg5xd8. Black then has the retort 7. . . . Bf8-b4+, forcing White to ditch his own queen at d2. After the queen's capture, Black's king completes the humiliation by meandering over to ingest the bishop on d8.

How, what, and why: Normally, White has no reason to fear the arrival of the Black bishop on b4, for the attack along the a5-e1 diagonal can be pitted in several ways, blocking at either c3 or d2 without repercussion. But in this situation, White's c-pawn and queen-knight are gone, and the dark-square bishop winds up out of position on d8. Remarkably, when Black checks on move seven, Bf8-b4, the only piece White can bar the check with is his queen! Since the White king has nowhere to go, the queen must do its chessic duty and surrender itself.

FRENCH DEFENSE   **1.** e4   e6   **2.** d4   d5   **3.** exd5   exd5
                     4. Nc3   Nf6   **5.** Qf3   Bd6   **6.** Be3

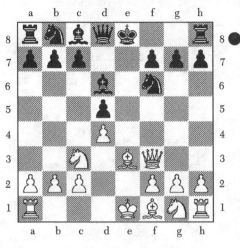

BLACK TO MOVE

Winning way: The seemingly ingenuous **6. . . . Bg4** is actually somewhat more deceptive than it appears. The development not only attacks the queen, it snares it for good.

How, what, and why: Go back one move from the position of the diagram, to White's sixth move. Why can't White take the d5-pawn, 6. Nc3xd5? The answer is that after 6. . . . Nf6xd5 7. Qf3xd5, Black checks on b4, uncovering a winning attack to White's queen. So White breathes a sigh of relief and plays the "safe" development 6. Bc1-e3, which in fact cuts down on the queen's horizontal maneuverability. In disbelief, White watches as his queen is lassoed by networking bishops. Instead of e3, a preferable place for the queen-bishop is g5. If Black then continues 6. . . . Bc8-g4, White rotates the table with 7. Bg5xf6!, winning a piece.

FRENCH DEFENSE   **1.** e4 e6   **2.** d4 d5   **3.** Nc3 Nf6
                     4. exd5 exd5   **5.** Qf3 Nc6   **6.** Be3 Nb4
                     7. 0-0-0

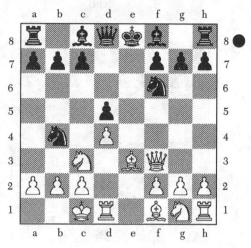

BLACK TO MOVE

Winning way: Black gains the exchange by the skewering **7. . . . Bg4.** Since the bishop is protected by the f6-knight, White's queen must decamp, and Black gains the exchange (here, a rook for a bishop) by taking on d1.

How, what, and why: The questions arise after Black's sixth move, when his knight invades, attacking the c2-pawn. The most natural response, castling queenside, loses the exchange to Bc8-g4. So how should White cope with the threat to c2? Any of three ways seem adequate. He could develop his king-bishop to d3, though that allows Black to exchange a knight for a bishop; he could shift the rook over to c1, though that renders queenside castling impossible; or he could retreat the queen to d1—but, sadly, this is a retreat. Clearly, Black gets the edge no matter how White plays, but White needn't lose the exchange.

129   Bg5 snares d8 and forces f7-f6

QUEEN PAWN OPENING   **1.** d4   Nf6   **2.** Nc3   e5
                        3. dxe5 Ng4   **4.** Nf3   Bc5
                        5. Ne4   Bb4+ **6.** c3   Ba5
                        7. h3   Nh6

WHITE TO MOVE

Winning way: White gnashes with **8. Bg5.** Black must block with the f-pawn to save his queen, 8. . . . f7-f6, but the queen remains endangered after 9. e5xf6. Since taking back loses the queen (9. . . . g7xf6 10. Bg5xf6), and with White threatening to take on g7 as well as to push to f7 with check, the position is resignable.

How, what, and why: Black gets his opening variations mixed up. There's an opening called the Budapest Counter Gambit (1. d4 Nf6 2. c4 e5), which is more or less playable. But the version Black adopts, with White's knight already on c3, is decidedly unsound. From the centralized square e4, the knight fulfills many of White's chessified aims. It defends f2, attacks c5, g5, and f6, and supports kingside action. If there's such a thing as a perfect knight, this is it.

GIUOCO PIANO **1.** e4 e5 **2.** Nf3 Nc6 **3.** Bc4 Bc5
4. d3 Nf6 **5.** Nc3 0-0 **6.** Bg5 h6
7. Bh4 Bb4 **8.** 0-0 Bxc3 **9.** bxc3 g5
10. Nxg5 hxg5 **11.** Bxg5 d6

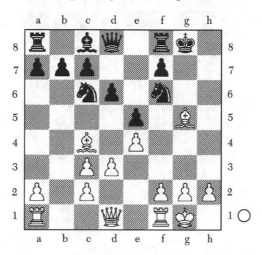

WHITE TO MOVE

Winning way: White turns up the heat with **12. f4,** and there's really no decent way to safeguard the f6-knight. The f-file is going to open and White will surely smash through.

How, what, and why: When Black attempts to break the pin on his f6-knight by advancing the g-pawn two squares, it poses a situation that typically perplexes the casual player: whether to sacrifice the knight (Nf3xg5) or to retreat the bishop (Bh4-g3). There are no easy answers, and the decision often comes down to how much follow-up pressure White can muster against f6. In this example we see one way to do it: to advance the f-pawn, trade it off, and open the f-file for the f1-rook. This doesn't always work, but after 12. f2-f4, Black is in trouble. The knight will go, for instance, after 12. . . . e5xf4 13. Rf1xf4.

GIUOCO PIANO **1.** e4 e5 **2.** Nf3 Nc6 **3.** Bc4 Bc5
4. 0-0 d6 **5.** d3 Bg4 **6.** Nc3 Nd4
7. h3

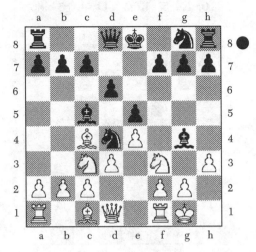

BLACK TO MOVE

Winning way: Black slams through and gains a pawn with **7. . . . Nxf3+**. The g-pawn must take back, abandoning the h3-pawn to oblivion, 8. . . . Bg4xh3. White's kingside is left full of holes.

How, what, and why: White is too slow in picking up the danger signs. By castling on move four, he allows Black to create the first pin. After establishing the pin, of course Black wants to pile pressure on the pinned unit. Thus White shouldn't allow Black's c6-knight an uncontested entry at d4. This invasion can be thwarted by 6. c2-c3, with White's queen-knight subsequently deploying to d2 instead of c3. White's actual advance, 7. h2-h3, kicking the bishop, is a loser. A better try is to admit his error, shifting his king from g1 to h1, so that after White takes back on f3 with the g-pawn, his rook can utilize the g-file, turning a weakness into a strength.

RUY LOPEZ **1.** e4 e5 **2.** Nf3 Nc6 **3.** Bb5 Nge7
              4. 0-0 d6 **5.** d3 Ng6 **6.** Nbd2 Qf6
              7. c3 Nf4 **8.** h3

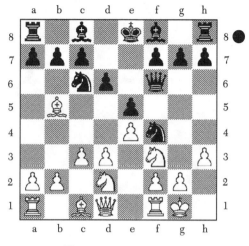

BLACK TO MOVE

Winning way: The kingside is ripped apart by **8. . . . Bxh3!**. If White defends himself by taking back, Black's queen check at g6 tells the true story. To stop mate, White will have to cede his queen.

How, what, and why: The heedless advance h2-h3 is clearly a mistake. After 8. . . . Bc8xh3 9. g2xh3 Qf6-g6+, to avoid mate at g2, White is reduced to throwing away a knight at g5. He actually loses his queen after 10. . . . Qg6xg5+ 11. Qd1-g4 Nf4xh3+. To avoid exposing his king, White mustn't take back on h3, which leaves Black in command. How did Black obtain such a powerful kingside assault? The answer lies in White's passive opening play. He's all geared up for the advance d2-d4, but doesn't play it. If you want to deter a flank attack, take action in the center and don't tarry.

THREE KNIGHTS GAME **1.** e4 e5 **2.** Nf3 Nc6 **3.** Nc3 g6
          4. d4 exd4 **5.** Nd5 Bg7
          6. Bg5 Nge7 **7.** Nxd4 Bxd4
          8. Qxd4 Nxd4

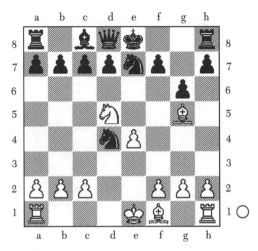

WHITE TO MOVE

Winning way: White could regain his queen by taking on e7 (Bg5x3e7), but better yet is **9. Nf6+.** After the compulsory move of Black's king to f8, the dark-square bishop mates at h6.

How, what, and why: This example is a close relative of Legal's Mate, where the queen is sacrificed to break a pin, resulting in mate by minor pieces. Because of the aggressive placement of White's forces, Black has to defend with careful steps. Surprisingly, he can live to tell his tale by blocking on e7 with the queen-knight (6. . . . Nc6-e7), the one already developed, instead of with the king-knight (6. . . . Ng8-e7), developing a new piece. By using the queen-knight (and violating a principle) he unblocks the c-pawn, which can then move to c6, clearing the logjam. Sometimes you have to break the rules in order to control them.

♛

CHAPTER TEN

Pieces and Pawns

The concluding chapter features seventeen examples. There are queenside underminings, queen traps, kingside bust-ups, and various snares with pawns, especially exploiting pieces that move to the edge or enter where they shouldn't. The most celebrated one is the Noah's Ark Trap of the Ruy Lopez (example 143), where three Black queenside pawns envelop White's light-square bishop. There are also several instances of the principle "a knight on the rim is grim," in which a simple pawn attack nails a knight on the perimeter. The section concludes with a surprise underpromotion.

Sicilian Defense   **1.** e4   c5   **2.** Nf3   Nc6   **3.** Bb5   g6
                4. Bxc6   bxc6   **5.** Nc3   Bg7   **6.** d3   d6
                7. Bg5   Rb8   **8.** Rb1

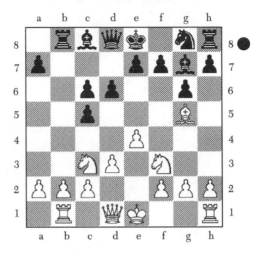

BLACK TO MOVE

Winning way: Black notches a pawn with **8. . . . Rxb2!**. If White takes back, the dark-square bishop captures the c3-knight with check, and then the b2-rook.

How, what, and why: Black's neat trick knocks the props out from under the c3-knight. Once b2 is destroyed, the g7-bishop sweeps away everything in its path. If White realized the full import of Black's 7. . . . Ra8-b8, he'd find some other way to protect b2. The only try that works is to position the White queen at c1. Then if Black's queen swings to a5, White can keep it together by drawing the queen-bishop back to d2. As a rule of thumb, whenever your opponent has a flanked bishop at g7, beware of trading pieces if it leads to the opening of the b-file. Once the opposing queen-rook slides to b8, the converging pressure against b2 can be debilitating.

Na4 traps the queen

MODERN DEFENSE   **1.** e4   d6   **2.** d4   g6   **3.** Nc3   Bg7

                             4. f4   c6   **5.** Be3   Qb6   **6.** a3   Qxb2

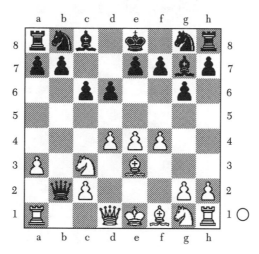

WHITE TO MOVE

Winning way: Black's queen threatens the c3-knight, but it doesn't have anywhere to go after **7. Na4.** Suddenly, the knight attacks the queen and deprives Her Majesty of her only retreat square, b6.

How, what, and why: It's a familiar story, getting into trouble by taking a poisoned pawn with the queen. A warning siren should go off when White advances a2-a3 on move six, ignoring Black's threat to capture the b2-pawn. Black should make sure that, if the queen enters the lion's den, there's a way to get out. Actually, the quiet pawn move a2-a3 is very crafty. If the pawn stays back on a2, Black's queen can exit at either a3 or b4. But by virtue of moving the a-pawn up one square, a3 is obstructed (and guarded by the a1-rook), and b4 is protected by the a3-pawn. That's a net, and the queen is trapped.

Bh6 piles on g7-pin

DANISH GAMBIT   **1.** e4 e5   **2.** d4 exd4   **3.** c3 dxc3
   4. Nxc3 Bb4   **5.** Qd4 Bxc3+
   6. Qxc3 Nf6   **7.** e5 Nd5   **8.** Qg3 0-0

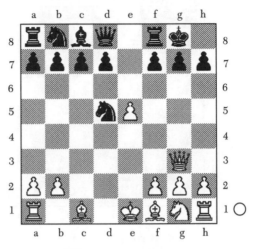

WHITE TO MOVE

Winning way: Black is castled, but White's bishop rudely intrudes with **9. Bh6!**. Mate is stopped by 9. . . . g7-g6, and White gobbles the exchange, 10. Bh6xf8.

How, what, and why: The threat to capture on g7 is serious. Black thinks he can handle it by castling, but that fails to Bc1-h6. Moreover, the push g7-g6 leaves the dark squares weak and prone to White's queen-bishop. Nor does sliding the king over to f8 help, for it renounces castling and keeps the king in a precarious state. The inescapable conclusion is that White is already on top. To find an improvement, we have to go back to move four, when Black plays a move with the king-bishop that leads to its exchange. It's the disappearance of this bishop that weakens the dark squares and entails subsequent problems. A better fourth move? Try developing the queen-knight to c6.

137 Rxh5 rips open kingside

PIRC DEFENSE
1. e4 d6 **2.** d4 Nf6 **3.** Nc3 g6
4. Bg5 Bg7 **5.** Qd2 0-0 **6.** Bh6 Nbd7
7. h4 c6 **8.** h5 Nxh5

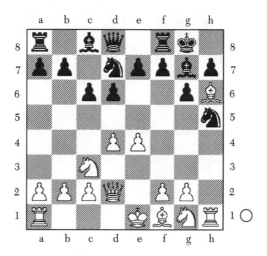

WHITE TO MOVE

Winning way: White strikes with **9. Rxh5,** clearly winning a piece. If Black recaptures, 9. . . . g6xh5, he gets mated via 10. Qd2-g5 and 11. Qg5xg7.

How, what, and why: In order to attack a fianchettoed castled position, three things must be dealt with: the defending pawn cover, the flanked bishop, and the king-knight. When White advances the rook-pawn to h5, and his rook captures Black's knight, two of these objectives are accomplished. The kingside pawn structure is broken up and the king-knight is eliminated. This leaves only the g7-bishop, and with the king-knight file exposed, White overcomes that easily by the crushing pin 10. Qd2-g5. With the h6-bishop already in place to pile on g7, there's no defense.

DANISH GAMBIT   **1.** e4 e5 **2.** d4 exd4 **3.** c3 dxc3
                4. Nxc3 Bb4 **5.** Qd4 c5 **6.** Qxg7 Qf6

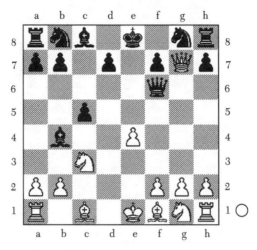

WHITE TO MOVE

Winning way: It looks like Black holds the fort, but there's a Trojan horse, **7. Bh6!**, menacing mate at f8. If Black trades queens, White's bishop corners the rook. And if 7. . . . c5-c4, to guard f8, White trades queens and then forks knight and rook by moving the bishop to g7.

How, what, and why: Both sides rely on x-ray defenses. Black's queen guards the h8-rook through the body of White's queen at g7, and White's queen provides an x-ray defense of c3 through Black's queen. The weird configuration is completed by the surreal entry of the bishop to h6. Neither Black's queen nor his g8-knight can take it without consequences. Nor does it help Black to insert a capture and check at c3. Again, the problems stem from Black's fourth move, which weakened the dark squares, most notably g7. A wiser course on move four is to develop the queen-knight to c6. At least it would be a game.

139   Bg6# gives criss-cross mate

FRENCH DEFENSE   **1.** e4 e6 **2.** d4 d5 **3.** Nc3 Bb4
4. Bd3 Bxc3+ **5.** bxc3 h6
6. Ba3 Nd7 **7.** Qe2 dxe4 **8.** Qxe4 Nf6

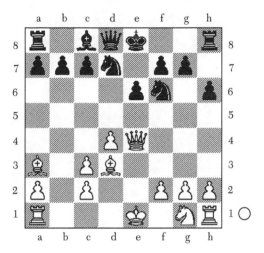

WHITE TO MOVE

Winning way: White's queen is threatened, but that only forces White to save the queen by giving it up in a pseudosacrifice, **9. Qxe6+!**. Either White mates at e7, or Black takes the queen, enabling the d3-bishop to mate at g6.

How, what, and why: A move like 5. . . . h7-h6 is usually played to prevent enemy pieces from coming to g5, but there are ramifications. The advance weakens g6. In this game, it even proves irrelevant because the c1-bishop ignores g5 for the rosy a3. The only thing that holds off the Vandals is the f7-pawn, which guards both g6 and e6. But White shows that it's overloaded by 9. Qe4xe6+!. This deflects the f7-pawn, and that's all the d3-bishop needs to complete the criss-crossing of bishops. Black's sixth and eighth moves didn't help, but it all started with that innocuous looking move, h7-h6.

Latvian Counter Gambit   **1.** e4   e5   **2.** Nf3   f5
                           3. Nxe5   Qf6   **4.** d4   d6
                           5. Nc4   fxe4   **6.** Be2   Qg6

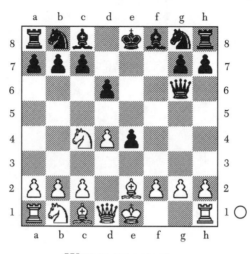

WHITE TO MOVE

Winning way: Black's king and queen are lined up on the same diagonal and there's no intervening f-pawn. It has all the trappings of a royal barbecue, with **7. Bh5** providing the sauce. Backed up by White's queen, the bishop pins Black's queen and wins it.

How, what, and why: Black is guilty of mechanical play. Nine times out of ten, Black shifts the queen to g6 in the Latvian with no ill effects. It's what happens, for instance, when White plays the main-line move 6. Nb1-c3, attacking the e4-pawn. But this is the tenth time, and White plays a different sixth move (Bf1-e2) expressly designed to keep Black's queen from its best square. By the time Black realizes this, it's too late. The queen is already pinned.

141   Bxh7+ is a classic bishop sac

FRENCH DEFENSE   **1.** e4   e6   **2.** d4   d5   **3.** Nc3   Bb4
                     4. Bd3   Nf6   **5.** e5   Nfd7   **6.** Nh3   0-0
                     7. Bxh7+   Kxh7   **8.** Qh5+   Kg8
                     9. Ng5   Re8

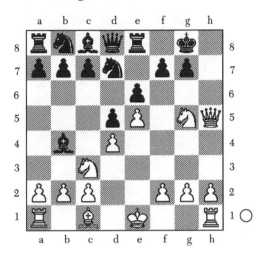

WHITE TO MOVE

Winning way: White finishes off the supposed opposition with **10. Qxf7+.** This produces forced mate by 10. . . . Kh8 11. Qh5+ Kg8 12. Qh7+ Kf8 13. Qh8+ Ke7 14. Qxg7#.

How, what, and why: The sequence starting with Bd3xh7+ is known as Greco's Classic Bishop Sacrifice. It dates back to the year 1619, and it's something every student should know. The length of the sequence is eight moves, which seems fairly long, and here it ends in mate. Black has two points where he can vary. He can dump the queen for the knight on g5, but that's also a loser. Also, Black can decline the initial bishop sacrifice on move seven, shifting his king to the corner. But Qd1-h5 comes in anyway, and it's a killer.

142   Ne7+ sets up rook and knight mate

RUY LOPEZ   **1.** e4 e5 **2.** Nf3 Nc6 **3.** Bb5 Nf6
         4. 0-0 Nxe4 **5.** Re1 Nd6 **6.** Nxe5 Nxe5
         7. Rxe5+ Be7 **8.** Nc3 Nxb5 **9.** Nd5 0-0
         10. Nxe7+ Kh8 **11.** Qh5 d6

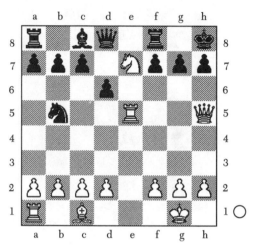

WHITE TO MOVE

Winning way: White is all geared up for the blow-'em-away sacrifice, **12. Qxh7+**. After Black takes back, White's rook mates at h5.

How, what, and why: Attempts to improve on Black's eleventh move do not bear fruit. If 11. . . . g7-g6, White replies 12. Qh5-h6, with the threat of 13. Re5-h5 g6xh5 14. Qh6-f6#. Moreover, defending by advancing the rook-pawn, 11. . . . h7-h6, invites 12. d2-d3 and 13. Bc1xh6. It turns out that Black has been on a downhill roller coaster for some time. The earliest he can stop it is move eight, when he can castle before White gets his knight to d5. But Black waits one move too long and can't get off the ride.

RUY LOPEZ   **1.** e4   e5   **2.** Nf3   Nc6   **3.** Bb5   a6
            4. Ba4   Nf6   **5.** 0-0   d6   **6.** d4   b5
            7. Bb3   Nxd4   **8.** Nxd4   exd4   **9.** Qxd4

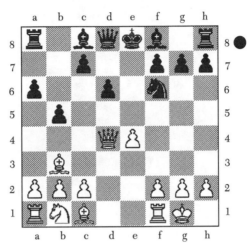

BLACK TO MOVE

Winning way: The simple advance of the c-pawn proves White's undoing. After **9. ... c5,** White's queen is attacked and must move to safety. No matter where it goes, Black's c-pawn moves in on the b3-bishop.

How, what, and why: White is in too great a hurry on move nine to regain the d4-pawn. The queen cannot maintain itself in the center, and its presence only encourages Black to mobilize the c-pawn, with fatal consequences for the b3-bishop. A better ninth move for White is Bb3-d5, which avoids the bishop's entrapment. Another idea is the promising gambit 9. c2-c3. In either case, the bishop escapes the coils of the Black c-pawn. This particular attack, where three Black queenside pawns surround White's light-square bishop, is so old and hoary it's acquired a name: the Noah's Ark Trap.

GIUOCO PIANO   **1.** e4   e5   **2.** Nf3   Nc6   **3.** Bc4   Bc5
                 4. c3   Nf6   **5.** d4   Bb6   **6.** d5   Na5
                 7. Bd3   d6

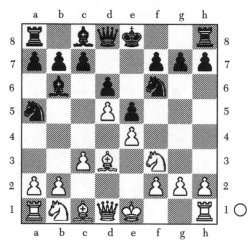

WHITE TO MOVE

Winning way: The simple thrust of the b-pawn **8. b4,** puts the Black knight in a predicament. It has nowhere safe to go, and White will collect it next move.

How, what, and why: At the edge of the board, a knight can have a maximum of four places to move. In our example, since b7 is already occupied by a Black pawn, that reduces the knight's options to three, and all three of those squares (b3, c4, and c6) are in White's camp. A crucial point is reached after White plays 6. d4-d5, attacking the c6-knight, which should retreat to b8 or shift to e7. But the square a5 looks tempting because it puts the knight in position to capture the c4-bishop. Once the bishop withdraws to d3, however, the knight is really out of it.

g4 traps Nh5

PIRC DEFENSE   **1.** e4   d6   **2.** d4   Nf6   **3.** Nc3   g6
4. f3   Bg7   **5.** Be3   0-0   **6.** Qd2   Re8
7. 0-0-0   Nbd7   **8.** e5   Nh5

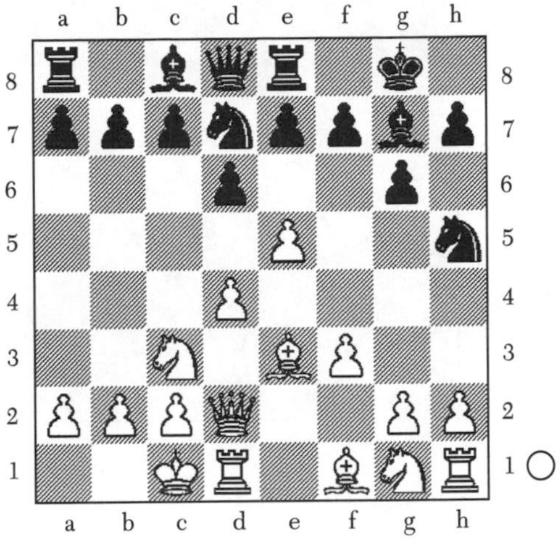

WHITE TO MOVE

Winning way: Another case of a knight on the edge, facing oblivion—this time, on the kingside. It's dead meat after **9. g4.**

How, what, and why: Black's seventh move (Nb8-d7) is inaccurate, especially when combined with his sixth move (Rf8-e8). Both these deployments take away possible maneuvering squares for the f6-knight, compelling it to move where no knight wants to go (the edge, with no accessible spots). A better seventh move for Black is to advance the c-pawn one square, to c6, keeping d7 clear and also guarding d5.

d6 traps Ne5

ENGLISH OPENING   **1.** c4   e5   **2.** Nf3   e4   **3.** Ne5

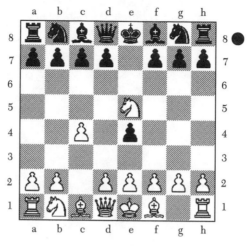

BLACK TO MOVE

Winning way: A knight on e5 can exert a powerful presence, striking in eight directions. But even a centralized stallion has to give way when attacked by a pawn. After **3. . . . d6,** the e5-knight is simply corralled.

How, what, and why: It's tempting to criticize White for his provocative second move, which encourages Black to advance his e-pawn. But, in fact, there is nothing wrong with it. White merely has to find a suitable place to put his knight. The squares h4 and g5 can be eliminated on sight, for Black's queen has an eye on them. And g1 is rejectable because of its passivity. So that leaves the center squares e5 and d4. With just a little foresight, White should have seen what's wrong with e5 and selected d4. But that's another game.

c6 blocks Bb5+ with tempo

OLD INDIAN DEFENSE **1.** Nf3 d6 **2.** e3 e5 **3.** d4 e4
4. Bb5+

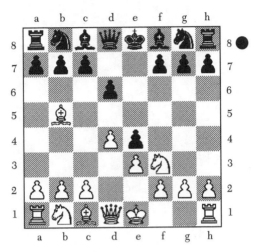

BLACK TO MOVE

Winning way: Black is in check, and the right way to get out of check is **4. . . . c6.** This threatens the bishop, and since White didn't bother to save his f3-knight, he must now drop one of two pieces, the bishop on b5 or the knight on f3.

How, what, and why: On move four, White should retreat his attacked knight to d2. But White sees the check on b5 and is drawn to it. Funny thing about checks—they're not all good. Sometimes they can be answered in a way that confers advantage on the defender, and that's what happens here. If one of your units is attacked, don't ignore the attack to issue a threat of your own unless you're sure you have a reasonable reply to your opponent's anticipated move. And if you're not certain what your opponent will do, it's better to save your own attacked unit. Answer your opponent's threats and you should be in decent shape.

PHILIDOR DEFENSE **1.** e4 e5 **2.** Nf3 d6 **3.** Bc4 c6
4. a4 Nf6 **5.** d3 Be7 **6.** Nc3 0-0
7. Be3

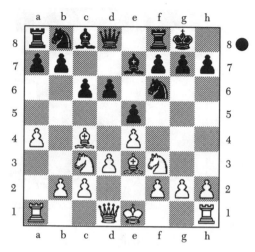

BLACK TO MOVE

Winning way: Black can capitalize on White's inharmonious development, starting with **7. . . . d5.** This gains time, and after 8. exd5 cxd5 9. Bb3, Black has a winning pawn fork at d4.

How, what, and why: It's easy to be lulled into a false sense of security by the solid and somewhat passive layout of Black's opening. If White's antennae were tuned, he'd pick up on the move c7-c6, a signal for latent aggression in the center. Then, instead of his fatal seventh move (Bc1-e3), he could substitute Bc4-b3, backing off to anticipate Black's d-pawn advance. Still another idea is to develop the queen-bishop to g5, where it could affect the square d5 by exchanging itself for the f6-knight. Both these ideas certainly confront Black's central expansion head-on.

RUY LOPEZ   **1.** e4   e5   **2.** Nf3   Nc6   **3.** Bb5   Bc5
             4. 0-0   d6   **5.** d4   Bb6

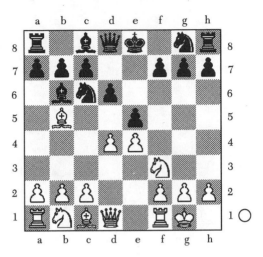

WHITE TO MOVE

Winning way: White could win a pawn by taking twice on e5, but he has something better. He should attack Black's pinned knight by **6. d5.** The best Black can do is a one-move attack to the b5-bishop (a7-a6), but after withdrawing to a4, the bishop maintains the pin and the knight falls.

How, what, and why: Black's fifth move, retreating the bishop to b6, is a mistake. For one, it doesn't answer White's threat to advance the d-pawn. Moreover, by placing the bishop on b6, Black obstructs his own b-pawn. This prevents the b-pawn from advancing to b5 to break the pin. Instead of retreating to b6, Black should trade pawns on d4, preferably playing 5. . . . e5xd4. Then on 6. Nf3xd4, Black secures c6 with 6. . . . Bc8-d7. If we only looked at the consequences of our actions, life would go so much more smoothly.

King's Gambit Accepted   **1.** e4   e5   **2.** f4   exf4
                          3. b3   Qh4+   **4.** g3   fxg3   **5.** h3

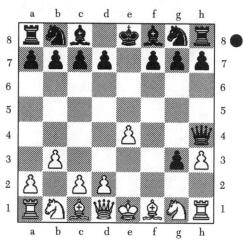

Black to move

Winning way: Black has several ways to win, but the quickest and best is **5. . . . g2+!**, which ends imaginatively after 6. Ke1-e2 Qh4xe4+ 7. Ke2-f2 g2xh1/N#!—mating by underpromoting to a knight.

How, what, and why: White plays a bunch of pawn moves, two of which lead to a debacle. The first mistake is 3. b2-b3, which has little to do with anything and permits the destructive check 3. . . . Qd8-h4+. The second error is to block on g3 with the g-pawn. Better to move the king to e2, trying to weather the storm. Finally, the advance 5. h2-h3 is a big loser, after which mate is forced. But at this point, even if White avoids mate, he still must lose a lot of material.

OPENINGS INDEX

Descriptive Names

(Numbers refer to examples.)

TACTICS INDEX

(Numbers refer to examples. Several tactics may apply to the same game.)

ACTIVE DEFENSE	7	16	48	49	65	147	
ATTRACTION/							
DEFLECTION	12	83	115	116	117	122	131
BATTERY	42	43	44	45	46	47	59	80
BUST-UP							
SACRIFICE	132	137					
CLEARANCE	10	11	24	25			
CORNERED							
ROOK	3	34	35	70	138	150	
DIRECT ATTACK	75						
DISCOVERY	4	18	27	33	57	66	84	85
	86	87	91	93	94	95	96	97
	98	99	100	101	102	103	104	105
	106	107	108	129	150		
DOUBLE ATTACK	15	17	24	25	38	39	41	42
	43	45	47	55	56	57	59	60
	66	67	68	100	115	147	
DOUBLE CHECK	106	107					
FOOL'S MATE	4	5	6	122	139		
FORCING KING							
TO MOVE	2	8	14	58	79	81	82	84
	89	90	91	92	93	114	120	
FORK	1	2	3	7	8	9	11	12

♛

INDEX OF LINES OF ATTACK

(Numbers refer to examples. Several lines of attack may be utilized during each game. For instance, Example 1 is listed under "e8-h5" [the e8-h5 diagonal] and "fifth rank," because White's actual winning move [Qh5] exploits both of these lines.)

DIAGONALS

a1-h8	17	35	39	55	69	70	116	134	138
a2-g8	18	36	38	40	41	42	44	45	47	49
	50	53	58	59	62	71	75	79	80	81
	82	83	90	91	92	94	97	111		
a3-f8	139								
a4-e8	13	19	20	21	22	25	29	30	33	87
	99	123	124	125	149				
a5-d8	14	74							
a5-e1	14	23	24	26	27	28	32	73	85	101
	107	115	117	118	120	126			
a7-g1	37	39	43	46	51	54	61	72	76	88
	89	93	95	96	103	104	116		
a8-h1	3	34	38	40	56	57	58	68	77	78
	81	102	110	150					
b1-h7	4	5	7	14	68	86	115	118	121	141
b8-h2	17	60	74						
c1-h6	64	133	137						
c8-h3	46	65	66	91	131	132			
d1-h5	92	94	97	98	100	127	128	140	

d8-h4	95	96	125	129	130					
e1-h4	3	6	12	16	122	150				
e8-h5	1	2	4	5	8	9	10	11	13	14
	15	18	139	140						
f8-h6	133	136	138							

FILES

a-file	20	30	31	32	33					
b-file	13	42	45	50	51	52	59	134		
c-file	82	113								
d-file	83	84	85	86	87					
e-file	17	70	73	105	106	107	108	109	111	112
	139	150								
f-file	56	58	79	91	130					
g-file	60	63	64	66	67	136	137	138		
h-file	16	72	137	141	142					

RANKS

third rank	53	59	62							
fourth rank	3	12	19	21	25	29	37	65	69	
fifth rank	1	2	9	10	11	13	14	15	17	23
	24	26	27	28	36	40	41	63	64	

ABOUT THE AUTHOR

Bruce Pandolfini is the author of more than twenty instructional chess books, including his most recent title, *Kasparov and Deep Blue: The Historic Chess Match Between Man and Machine.* In his new video, *Chess Starts Here,* he teams up with former student Josh Waitzkin to provide a novel way to introduce chess basics. A professional chess teacher since the Fischer-Spassky match of 1972, Pandolfini has seen his favorite game break new grounds, from the keyboards of computer scientists to the classrooms of America and the world. At his own chessboard, he says he can't stop teaching because there's still too much to learn.